BUG CAMP

Where Every Day's an ADVENTURE

Tim Forrest, PhD & Jen Hamel, PhD

Quarto is the authority on a wide range of topics.
Quarto educates, entertains, and enriches the lives of our readers—
enthusiasts and lovers of hands-on living.
www.quartoknows.com

MoonDance

6 Orchard Road, Suite 100
Lake Forest, CA 92630
quartoknows.com
Visit our blogs at quartoknows.com

Printed in China
1 3 5 7 9 10 8 6 4 2

MIX
Paper from
responsible sources
FSC® C101537

CONTENTS

Welcome to BUG CAMP!

Insects rule! In the 400 million years since their humble beginnings as simple, wingless, soil-dwelling arthropods, insects have evolved powerful flight and complex metamorphosis. In other words, insects took off and transformed the earth! Insects now fill nearly every ecological niche and are the dominant animals in nearly every environment except oceans, where their crustacean cousins reign. Nearly 80 percent of the planet's animals are insects.

Some people, adults included, are afraid of insects or think insects are gross and disgusting. Once you stop and look closely, you will find that insects do some amazing things. The bizarre lifestyles and intriguing features of these six-legged creatures will grab your attention and make you think about connections in the world around you.

In the Internet age, many kids know more about animals on other continents than they do about those in their own backyard. **BUG CAMP** hopes you will discover the world just outside your back door. Learn cool tricks for

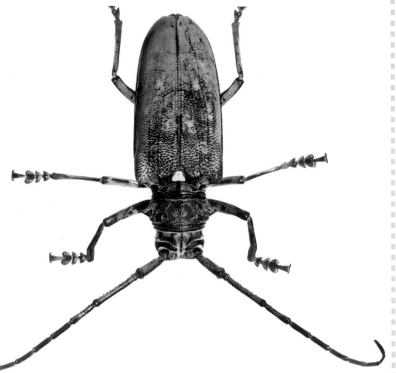

catching, collecting, and keeping insects. Search for insects in logs, ponds, and streams. See the fascinating insects that inhabit cow pies or roadkill. **BUG CAMP** is full of adventures where you are a scientist. Set up your own research lab to investigate how insects walk on water, measure the pulling strength of beetles, or change the daily singing rhythms of crickets. Study predators as you handfeed antlions, praying mantids, and water scorpions. Learn about pollinators and test their color vision.

BUG CAMP wants you to explore the world of insects, and hopes you will ask "why" as you spend time with these captivating animals. Come to **BUG CAMP** and have some fun. We know we will!

**It's time for
ADVENTURE!**

Jim Forrest   Jen Hamel

Hello,
INSECTS!

Zoologists like to organize animals based on their relationships with one another. They use similarities in body design to arrange animals into groups called taxa. For example, all animals with exoskeletons, segmented bodies, and jointed legs are grouped together and are called arthropods.

Think about exoskeletons, segmented bodies, and jointed legs for a minute. Can you list animals that would be classified as arthropods? Compare an earthworm, a dog, and a katydid. Do they have body segments? Exoskeletons? Jointed legs?

Arthropods

Insects are arthropods! So are spiders and crabs. Insects, spiders, and crabs share the characteristics of all arthropods, such as jointed appendages, but they also have differences that separate them into other groups. Can you think of any differences that would separate insects and spiders into different groups?

Insects

All insects are grouped together because they have three body regions: a head, a thorax with six jointed legs, and an abdomen. Insects also have one pair of antennae. Spiders are grouped together with other arachnids (scorpions and ticks) because they all have two body parts: a cephalothorax with eight jointed legs and an abdomen. Arachnids do not have antennae.

USING DEVICES AS MICROSCOPES

Because insects are small, it may be difficult to see all of an insect's body parts. You can use a microscope app on a phone or tablet to see insects in more detail.

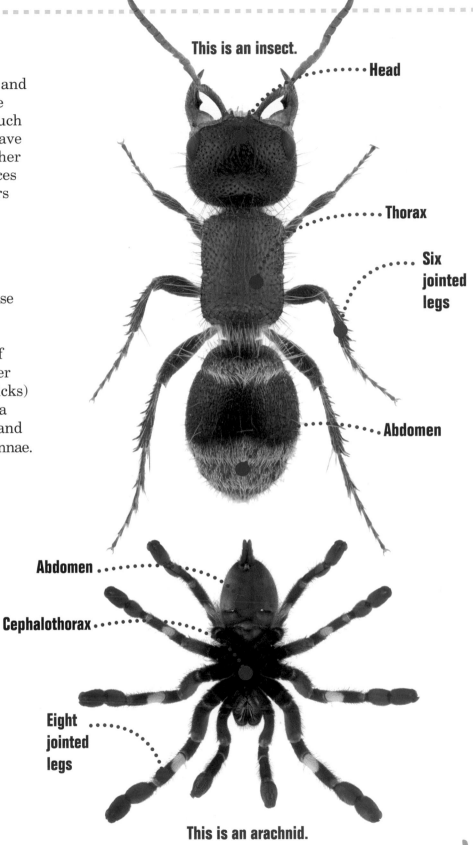

This is an insect.

Head

Thorax

Six jointed legs

Abdomen

Abdomen

Cephalothorax

Eight jointed legs

This is an arachnid.

Although many insects have ears for hearing, none has ears on its head! Instead, you can find ears on their legs, wings, antennae, abdomens, and thoraxes.

The Head

Like most animals, an insect's head has sense organs for tasting, smelling, seeing, and feeling. Insect heads may be very different looking but they all have the same general features: compound eyes, one pair of antennae, and mouthparts. They may also have simple eyes.

ANTENNAE
Insects use their antennae to smell. Insect antennae come in many shapes and sizes.

Simple eye

Compound eye

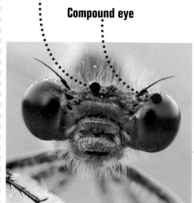

Stylate antennae are finger-like. Look for them on horse flies.

Aristate antennae are shaped like a bulb with a bristle. You can find them on house flies.

Setaceous antennae look like bristles. You can find them on dragonflies and damselflies.

Geniculate antennae are elbowed. Look for them on ants.

Plumose antennae are feather-like. Moths and midges have them.

Filiform antennae have a thread-like shape. Some beetles and cockroaches have them.

Lamellate antennae have a group of long plates that look like fans at the ends. Some beetles have them.

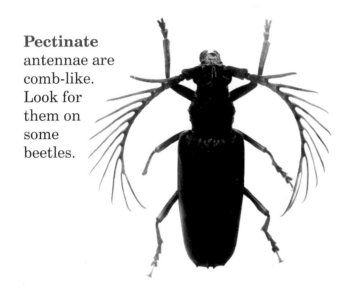

Pectinate antennae are comb-like. Look for them on some beetles.

Capitate antennae get wider at their tips. Look for them on butterflies.

MOUTHPARTS
The type of mouthparts an insect has depends on the food it eats.

Chewing mouth-parts are used for feeding on solid foods such as plants or animals. You can find them on grass-hoppers and many beetles.

Siphoning mouthparts are like a coiled drinking straw. Butterflies and moths use them to feed on liquids.

Sponging mouthparts are used to soak up liquid foods. Look for them on flies.

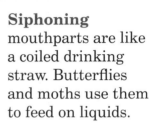

Piercing-Sucking mouthparts work like a needle in a doctor's office when the doctor draws blood. They are used to break into a food source and suck liquid from it. You can find them on mosquitoes and true bugs.

Chewing-Lapping mouthparts are used for eating solids and liquids. Look for them on bees.

The Thorax

The thorax of an insect is its motor. It has three segments, and each segment has a pair of jointed legs attached at the sides.
Look at an insect. Can you see the three segments with their legs attached? Some insects also have two or four wings that are attached to the second and third thoracic segments.

Legs

Most insects have legs with five segments that they use to walk and run.

These legs are called **cursorial** legs.

Some insect legs have adaptations in one or more of the five segments that help them do other jobs.

Fossorial legs are used for digging. Look for them on mole crickets and dung beetles.

Fossorial legs are like shovels.

Saltatorial legs are used for jumping. Grasshoppers, crickets, and katydids have them.

Raptorial legs are used for grasping. Look for them on praying mantises.

Natatorial legs are used for swimming. You can find them on diving beetles and water bugs.

Natatorial legs work like oars on a boat.

Raptorial legs are great grabbers.

Wings

Most insects have two pairs of wings on the thorax. In some groups, the wings have adapted from simple membranes.

Elytra are hard, thick front wings that cover and protect the thin back wings. You can find them on beetles and earwigs.

Hemelytra are leathery near the body and paper-like near the tip. Look for them on true bugs.

Halteres are knob-like hind wings adapted for balance and steering in flight. You can find them on house flies. To see halteres, check out the fly on the bottom right of page 18.

Tegmina are leathery front wings. You can find them on roaches, crickets, grasshoppers, and mantids.

Scaly wings are covered in small scales. Look for them on moths and butterflies.

The scales on butterfly wings are so small you need a microscope to see them. If you touch a butterfly wing, some scales will come off on your fingers and will look like dust.

The Abdomen

The abdomen of an insect is the best place to see its segments. Each segment may have a small opening on the sides. These openings are called spiracles and insects use them to breathe. The spiracles connect to small tubes called tracheae that bring oxygen to every part of the body.

Some insects have a pair of cerci (ser SEE) at the tip of their abdomen. They act like rear-end antennae, or as pincers, like earwigs have.

Cerci

Female insects may also have an ovipositor at the tip of their abdomen. Ovipositors are used to lay eggs — check out page 36 to see a cricket's ovipositor.

INSECT TAXA

Now you know the traits that all insects share: head, thorax, abdomen, six legs, and one pair of antennae. You also know some of the terms entomologists use to describe insect body parts. For example, ants have geniculate antennae, but katydids have filiform antennae.

You will need a few more tools if you want to identify some of the estimated six million (!) insect species. How do scientists classify and organize so many species? Entomologists have historically sorted insects into groups based on the way different body parts look. What kinds of things have you sorted into groups? Candy? Game cards? Piles of change?

Sorting can be a useful way to figure out how many different kinds of insects are

in a group. Grouping insects by how they look can also tell us how they are related. Closely related species often look more alike than distantly related species, but not always. Today, DNA can also tell us about relationships between insect groups.

In the next few pages, you will meet some of the major insect taxa, or big groups of species. The family tree that follows them shows how they are related and where some important insect traits evolved.

BUG Talk

Learning a few vocabulary words can help you have more insect adventures.

Entomologist: A biologist who studies insects

Metamorphosis: The changes in an individual's body form during its life cycle

Simple metamorphosis: In insects, the life cycle involving three stages where the young look similar to the adults

Complete metamorphosis: In insects, the life cycle involving four stages where the young look and act very different from adults and go through a transitional stage called the pupa

Nymph: Young stage of terrestrial insects with simple metamorphosis; often similar to adult in appearance and eats the same foods.

Naiad: A gill-bearing nymph of aquatic insects with simple metamorphosis

Larva: Young stage of insects with complete metamorphosis; their habits, appearance, and feeding are often very different from those of adults. **Larvae** is the plural form.

Pupa: Stage of insects with complete metamorphosis during the transition between larva and adult. **Pupae** is the plural form.

Juvenile: An insect nymph, naiad, or larva

Zygentoma, also known as Thysanura (silverfish): This is one of the oldest insect groups, and the first insects looked like them. Silverfish hatch from eggs, molt several times as juveniles, and continue molting as adults. Juveniles look a lot like adults.

How to Know If It's a Silverfish: Adults are covered in silver scales and do not have wings. Each silverfish has three "tails" coming off the abdomen: a middle filament and two cerci, one on each side. Silverfish have long, threadlike antennae, chewing mouthparts, and cursorial legs.

Collecting Tips: Silverfish live in dark, damp places. Outside, look under leaves and rocks. Inside, look in basements, kitchens, bathrooms, and storage boxes. They like to chew on paper and cardboard.

Odonata (dragonflies and damselflies): Odonates were the first insects with wings, and they are master predators of the air. The nymphs are called naiads. They develop underwater and look very different from adults. Like adults, naiads eat insects, but they also eat earthworms, snails, and even tadpoles and fish. Naiads crawl up out of the water and

hang on plants when they are ready to molt into adults. If you check the plants around the edge of a pond, you may find the shed exoskeleton of a naiad that molted into an adult!

How to Know If It's an Odonate: Adult dragonflies and damselflies are large and often brightly colored. They have long, thin abdomens and four large, long wings. They are strong fliers. Dragonflies and damselflies capture prey with their legs, which act like hanging baskets in flight. They have short antennae that look like bristles, and large, toothed mandibles. (Odonata means toothed one.) They use their large, compound eyes to find prey and mates, and to avoid predators such as people with nets!

Dragonflies and damselflies belong to two distinct groups. All dragonflies are more closely related to each other than they are to any damselflies.

How to Tell a Dragonfly from a Damselfly: While resting, dragonflies hold their wings out to the side, while damselflies hold their wings over their backs. Go to a pond and see if you can tell dragonflies from damselflies.

Collecting Tips: You can find adult dragonflies near water but they are hard to catch. Males are territorial and often land on the same perch or fly the same route. Watch what they do, wait nearby, and get ready to swing your net!

Adventures with Odonates: pages 60 and 61

Blattodea (roaches and termites): Roaches and termites have chewing mouthparts and cursorial legs.

How to Know If It's a Roach: Roaches have flat, oval bodies, tegmina, and filiform antennae.

The cerci on the ends of their bodies are very good at feeling air currents, which is why roaches are so good at getting away from people trying to squash them! A plate called a pronotum covers most of the roach's head and thorax. Roaches are scavengers and will eat almost anything.

How to Know If It's a Termite: Termites can look a little like ants. Unlike ants, their bodies are soft and light colored, and their antennae are straight. (Ant antennae are elbowed.) Termites live in colonies, like ants and many bees do. All the termites in a colony are very closely related, but some look very different from others because they have different jobs. Workers and soldiers do not have wings or eyes. They search for food and dig tunnels, and they tell each other about food they find with chemicals called pheromones (FAIR monz) that travel through the tunnels. Soldiers protect the colony. Workers feed soldiers. (Soldiers cannot feed themselves because their mandibles are too big!) The king and queen are the only termites with wings, and use them to swarm in mating flights.

Collecting Tips: For roaches, look in mulch and leaf litter. For roaches and termites too, look in decaying logs.

Adventures with Blattodeans: pages 91 and 92

Bug Camp Science

Grouping insects by what they look like often helps scientists understand which insects are closely related, but not always. Roaches and termites used to be in separate groups. Recently, scientists who study insect evolution used the genes from a lot of different insect species to draw a new family tree. These genes showed that termites and roaches are each others' closest relatives.

Many scientists now group termites and roaches together in Blattodea. However, if you look at books or Internet sources published before 2015, you'll probably see termites under their old name, Isoptera. This is something that is really cool about science: as scientists learn new things, the books change. If you pay attention, you'll see this happen with all kinds of science knowledge!

Mantodea (praying mantises): A praying mantis is an ambush predator! They wait for prey to come to them. They are usually well camouflaged.

How to Know If It's a Praying Mantis:
Mantids have strong, raptorial front legs for catching and holding on to prey, broad heads with large compound eyes, and strong chewing mouthparts. Mantids also have a long thorax, which allows them to turn their head to look over their "shoulder."

Adults have tegmina covering their thin, delicate hindwings. Both wings fold up and lie flat when mantids are not flying. Females are larger than males, and lay eggs in hard cases that they glue to small branches or plant stems.

Collecting Tips: Egg cases are often found on the ends of low plant branches and at the edges of fields. You can keep an egg case in a covered plastic container and wait for the mantids to hatch. Feed them small flies or they will eat each other!

Phasmatodea (stick insects): Walking sticks are masters of disguise! Stick insects have some of the strangest and longest body shapes in the insect world. The nymphs look a lot like adults.

How to Know If It's a Stick Insect: North American species look like sticks. They can also be shaped like leaves or other parts of plants. Stick insects feed on plants with

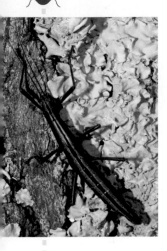

chewing mouthparts, and usually do not have wings.

Some stick insects protect themselves from vertebrates with chemicals. For example, the two-striped walking stick may spray if disturbed. Many stick insects don't just look like plants. They behave like them, too. They walk very slowly while swaying back and forth, just like a twig or leaf swaying in a gentle breeze.

Collecting Tips: Look on tree trunks and other large plants. Collect them at night because that's when they are active. These are large, slow insects, so hand-picking works well. Don't put your face up close to them because some can spray.

Orthoptera (grasshoppers, crickets, and katydids): These are the insect singers! Grasshoppers, crickets, and katydids all have body parts for making and hearing sounds.

How to Know If It's an Orthopteran: Orthopterans have saltatorial hind legs for jumping. Most adults have wings. Their wide, delicate hindwings fold under their tegmina. Orthopterans also all have filiform antennae.

Grasshopper antennae are shorter than their thorax, while crickets and katydids have long

antennae. Most orthopterans feed on plants with chewing mouthparts. Nymphs look like adults but do not have wings.

Collecting Tips: Walk slowly through a field with a net and grasshoppers will jump in front of you. If you see a katydid or cricket, you can use a net or vial to catch it. You might have better luck finding katydids and crickets by listening for them in the evening . . . just follow the sound.

Adventures with Orthopterans: pages 36, 37, 88, 89, and 92

Hemiptera (cicadas, hoppers, aphids, scale insects and true bugs): Like the Orthoptera, this group also has some impressive noisemakers. Cicadas are some of the loudest insects. Their close relatives, the hoppers, make interesting signals that travel through the stems of the plants they live and feed on. It takes special sensors to pick up hopper signals.

How to Know If It's a Hemipteran: All hemipterans have piercing-sucking mouthparts and a large "nose" that houses the inner pump that creates the suction they need to eat their liquid diets. Many also have a triangular shape, called the scutellum, on their backs where their front wings come together. Hemiptera contains a subgroup called the true bugs. True bugs have special front wings called hemelytra that are thickened and leathery at the base, but thin and delicate near the tip. Examples of true bugs are stink bugs, assassin bugs, squash bugs, toad bugs, and bed bugs. It is scientifically correct to call any insect with hemelytra a BUG.

Adult dobsonflies have large, flexible bodies, big chewing mouthparts, and long, filiform antennae. Adult males use long, pointy mandibles to fight with other males. Adult fishflies look like dobsonflies with smaller mouthparts. Male fishflies have plumose antennae. Alderflies are smaller than dobsonflies and fishflies. Adults are usually found near water. Females lay their eggs on rocks above the water (dobsonflies), grass stems (alderflies), or on leaves (fishflies).

Collecting Tips: Search near streetlights at night in the summer or near a stream or river. Use a plastic vial, net, or sealable lunch bag to catch them. To find dobsonfly eggs, look for round white patches on bridges or boulders at the stream edge. When the eggs hatch, the larvae drop into the water to start their predatory larval stage. Dobsonfly larvae are called hellgrammites and they may spend up to three years living in streams.

Collecting Tips: You can find hemipterans in just about every habitat. Look for toe-biters and water scorpions in water, and treehoppers, aphids, stink bugs, leaf-footed bugs, and cicadas on plants. You can hand-pick many of these insects, but be careful: some predators such as wheel bugs can bite or pinch.

Adventures with Hemipterans: pages 26, 38, and 59

Megaloptera (dobsonflies, alderflies, and fishflies): These large insects have thin wings with lots of easy-to-see veins.

How to Know If It's a Megalopteran: Unlike stoneflies and mayflies, these insects have no tails (cerci). Adults have four large narrow, delicate wings. The forewings and hindwings are about the same size. When not flying, they hold their wings over their bodies like a roof.

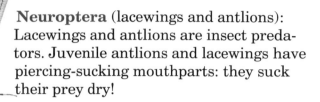

Neuroptera (lacewings and antlions): Lacewings and antlions are insect predators. Juvenile antlions and lacewings have piercing-sucking mouthparts: they suck their prey dry!

How to Know If It's a Neuropteran:

Adults in this group have four delicate wings with many branching veins. When not flying, the wings form a roof over their bodies. Adult antlions look a little like damselflies, but they have medium-long capitate antennae instead of setaceous antennae. Lacewing adults have ears on their wings.

Be on the Lookout:

Green lacewing larvae are slow-moving predators that disguise themselves with bits of lichen on their bodies. They can creep right into the middle of a group of aphids or treehoppers and feed without being noticed. If you see a little clump of walking lichen, it's probably a lacewing larva.

Adventures with Neuropterans:
pages 56 and 57

Coleoptera (beetles): Of all the insect groups, Coleoptera includes the most species — more than 400,000 species! Beetles can be tiny (less than 1 mm) or very large (more than 10 cm [4 inches]).

How to Know If It's a Beetle:
The name Coleoptera means "sheath wing," which refers to their elytra. When closed, these hard, often-shiny wings on the beetle's back often have a straight line between them. A beetle's hindwings are thin and delicate, and fold up underneath the elytra. Beetles have chewing mouthparts and cursorial legs. Their antennae come in many shapes and sizes. Beetle larvae are called grubs. Grubs come in different shapes, but often look like pale caterpillars with six legs.

Collecting Tips: You can find beetles anywhere: on plants, in the soil, in the water, in logs, in carrion, and even in poop. Hand-picking works well for many species, and so does a net. Many beetles come to lights.

Adventures with Coleopterans: pages 26, 35, 66, 67, and 80

Diptera (true flies): This large group contains about 120,000 species.

How to Know If It's a Fly: Count the wings! Flies only have two wings, or one pair. The hind wings of true flies are small knobs called halteres that help with balance and steering. Most flies are small with soft bodies and sucking mouthparts. Some flies have sponging mouthparts, though, and some have none. The small, wormlike larvae are called maggots.

Collecting Tips: Use a net or try a trap with a stinky bait such as dung or meat. Also, many flies are pollinators so you can find them near flowers.

Adventures with Dipterans: pages 24, 41, 66, and 67

Bug Camp Trivia

LOTS of insects have the word **"fly"** as part of their name. How many can you think of (stonefly, dragonfly, caddisfly . . .)? NONE of these insects is a true fly! If an insect name has "fly" in it, but "fly" is not a separate word, then the insect is not in Diptera. For example, dragonflies are odonates, but house flies are dipterans.

Lepidoptera (butterflies, moths, and skippers): The name Lepidoptera refers to the small scales covering the wings, abdomens, and legs of these insects. Some scales are brightly colored.

How to Know If It's a Lepidopteran: Each adult has a proboscis and large compound eyes. The shapes of antennae and bodies differ between moths, skippers, and butterflies.

Lepidopteran larvae are called caterpillars. They have soft bodies, with small legs attached to both the thorax and abdomen. The legs on the abdomen are called prolegs. Caterpillars use chewing mouthparts to feed on plants. Caterpillar bodies are soft and they move slowly, and many birds, bats, and other animals feed on them. Some caterpillars have patterns that make them look like snakes or other predators; others have patterns that help them hide.

Collecting Tips: USE A NET! Butterflies and skippers seem so easy to catch . . . until you try! Moths often come to lights. Some caterpillars defend themselves with special hairs that release venom — don't touch!

Adventures with Lepidopterans: pages 38–40, 66, and 67

Don't touch the fuzzy ones!

19

Hymenoptera
(sawflies, wasps, ants, and bees):
This is a large group of predators, pollinators, and parasites. Many species feed and care for their larvae and live in large groups or colonies.

How to Know If It's a Hymenopteran:
Bees, ants, and wasps have waists: their bodies pinch in near where the thorax and abdomen come together. Sawflies do not have waists. Sawflies, wasps, and bees all have four thin wings. Ants are like termites in that only reproducing queens and drones can fly. Reproducing ants have four thin wings, just like bees and wasps. The top and bottom wing on each side attach to each other with a row of tiny hooks called hamuli. Because of the

hamuli, the forewings and hindwings beat together when a bee flies. Sawflies, ants, and wasps have chewing mouthparts, and bees have mouthparts that can both chew and lap up nectar. Many ants, bees, and wasps have special ovipositors called stingers that release venom.

Collecting Tips: Use a net for bees and wasps and a pooter for ants. Remember that bees and wasps go UP, so don't put your face over the net when you open it!

Adventures with Hymenopterans:
pages 66, 67, 86, and 87

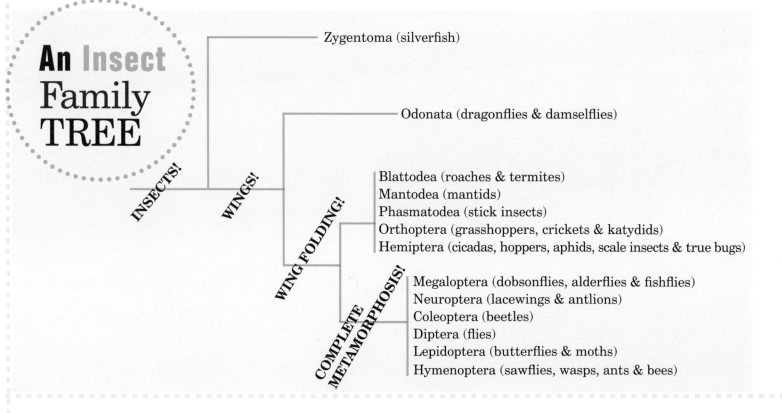

An Insect Family TREE

INSECTS!

WINGS!

WING FOLDING!

COMPLETE METAMORPHOSIS!

Zygentoma (silverfish)

Odonata (dragonflies & damselflies)

Blattodea (roaches & termites)
Mantodea (mantids)
Phasmatodea (stick insects)
Orthoptera (grasshoppers, crickets & katydids)
Hemiptera (cicadas, hoppers, aphids, scale insects & true bugs)

Megaloptera (dobsonflies, alderflies & fishflies)
Neuroptera (lacewings & antlions)
Coleoptera (beetles)
Diptera (flies)
Lepidoptera (butterflies & moths)
Hymenoptera (sawflies, wasps, ants & bees)

Insect METAMORPHOSIS & LIFECYCLES

Look at the family tree of insect taxa on the bottom of page 20. The earlier branches of the tree on the left side show events that happened earlier in time. Notice that silverfish (Thysanura) is on one of the first branches. Silverfish are primitive insects and do not have wings. They do not undergo metamorphosis at all! Insects with this kind of life cycle hatch from eggs into juveniles that look just like small adults. When there is no change in body form during the insect's life cycle, it is called ametabolous metamorphosis.

Many kinds of insects change in dramatic ways as they develop into adults. Although not all adult insects have wings, *only* adult insects have wings. In other words, if you see wings on an insect, it is an adult! Insects that have wings go through metamorphosis when their juvenile stages molt into adults. Look at the family tree again. Can you name the insect groups with metamorphosis? What about dragonflies (Odonata)? Grasshoppers (Orthoptera) or bugs (Hemiptera)? These insects have three life stages: egg, nymph (or naiad, if the nymph lives in water), and adult. Insects with three life stages have simple or hemimetabolous metamorphosis. Often, but not always, the nymphs look a lot like the adults.

 Nymph   **Adult**

Now look at the taxa on the last branch of the family tree. These groups include flies (Diptera), beetles (Coleoptera), and butterflies (Lepidoptera). In all of the taxa on this branch, the adult insects look very different from the young insects. Think about caterpillars and butterflies: they look very different from each other, even when they are of the same species! How does this happen? When an insect such as a fly or butterfly develops, it goes through four life stages (egg, larva, pupa, adult). The pupa is the stage where the amazing changes happen. Life cycles with a pupal stage have complete or holometabolous metamorphosis.

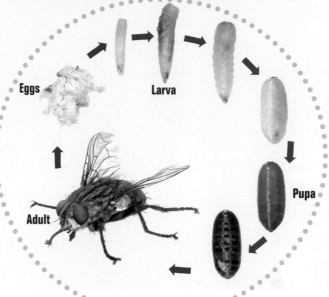

Insect GROWTH

Just like people, insects grow and develop from being kids (or juveniles) into adults. However, some of the things that happen to insects as they develop are very different from what happens to you.

Think about It: What happens to your clothes when you grow? Have you outgrown clothes you really liked? Like your clothing, an insect's exoskeleton cannot grow or expand. Because of this, when an insect grows, it sometimes needs to molt, or shed, its exoskeleton. After an insect molts, its exoskeleton is soft and takes a while to harden. Juvenile insects usually molt several times before becoming adults.

INSECT HABITATS

Insects seek out many places to make their homes and raise their young. Some of their choices may surprise you.

Logs

Dead and decaying wood attracts a host of insects and other animals. If you find a fallen tree in the forest, start by peeling away the bark and looking for insects. If the log is small enough, you might be able to roll it over and look under it.

You can use a screwdriver or a pry bar to get into the middle of the log where you might find the galleries of wood-boring insects such as termites, ants, wood roaches, bess bugs, and some beetle larvae. Centipedes, millipedes, and springtails are often found in logs, too.

Log-loving arthropods pictured here include a wood roach (far left), springtails (above left), a bess bug (above right), an earwig and her young (bottom left), and an ant (below).

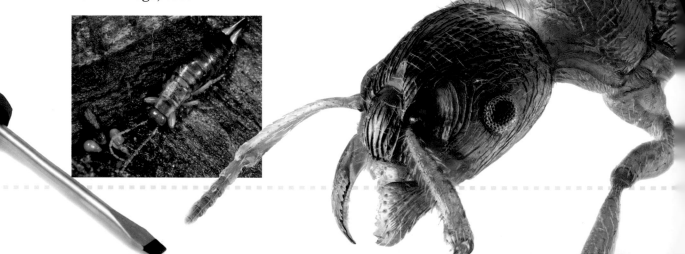

Leaf LITTER

You will be amazed at the number of animals you find in leaf litter. And, they are easy to collect with a Berlese funnel! You can learn how to make and use a Berlese funnel on pages 45 and 46. Most animals living in leaf litter are very small so you may need to use a microscope or hand lens to see them. You are likely to find small insects, springtails, psuedoscorpions, mites, other arachnids, and more.

Arthropods found in leaf litter include a mite (top right), a springtail (middle right), and a larval beetle (bottom right).

CARRION (dead animals)

Road trips to see carrion can be fun for bug collectors because dead animals attract many kinds of insects. The easiest place to find carrion is alongside roads. It is a good idea to use a stick to move carcasses away from the roadside so you can check them out away from traffic.

Carcasses go through very specific stages as they decompose. You will find different kinds and stages of insects on them, depending on how long the animal has been dead.

Have Fun Attracting Insects

You can attract your own insects using scraps of raw meat (chicken works well) or bones. Place the meat scraps on soil and leaf litter in a plastic container. Wash your hands well after handling the meat.

Put the container outside and watch what happens. Depending on where you live, you may need to put the container in a small cage or cover it loosely with wire mesh (at least 13-mm [½ inch] wide) to keep dogs, cats, and other animals from disturbing your carcass.

It should not take long before green bottle flies (a type of carrion fly) begin to arrive at the carcass and lay eggs. Insects you are likely to see are carrion flies (early), carrion beetles (later), and rove beetles (last). Record the different kinds of insects and when they arrive in a notebook.

Photos from top to bottom: a green bottle fly, a flesh fly, a carrion beetle, and finally, the rove beetle

Ponds

Pond water is usually warmer than moving stream water, and warmer water has less oxygen. Pond insects tend to be more active swimmers because they do not have to worry about stream currents. They may also have special body parts and behaviors for getting oxygen.

Below are a few examples of insects you are likely to find as you search in and around lakes and ponds. You may also find water scorpions, toe biters, and dragonfly naiads in ponds. (See pages 58–61 to learn more about them.)

Diving Beetles

Diving beetles are always fun to collect and watch. They are fast swimmers that use their hind legs as oars to paddle through water. When they dive, they carry a bubble of air under their wings. Just like a scuba tank, the air bubble helps the beetles breathe underwater. When they return to the surface, they get another air bubble.

Back Swimmers

These pond insects are named for their unusual behavior of swimming upside down! Like the diving beetles, their hind legs are excellent oars, helping them swim fast. If you look at their undersides when they are underwater, you will see a shiny, silvery bubble held in small hairs.

As with the diving beetles, this bubble lets the backswimmers breathe. These insects prey on other aquatic insects. They suck the prey's body juices with piercing and sucking mouthparts. Be careful when handling backswimmers . . . they bite!

Striders

Water striders walk on water. Have you ever wondered how they do this? Water has a high surface tension and water striders use it to hold themselves up. Look at a strider on water and notice the small dimples in the water where its legs touch the water. To move, striders push their legs against the water, which helps them skate across the surface.

Beetle is getting more air.

Diving beetles carry bubbles of air under their wings. The air bubbles help the beetles breathe underwater.

Bug Camp Experiment

Sinking Striders

Have you ever noticed that you can fill a cup of water a little bit above its rim? Surface tension explains why this happens.

You can change the surface tension of water with a small drop of soap. Place a water strider in a container of water and watch it skate across the surface. Notice the dimples in the water surface and notice which legs are used to propel the animal. What happens when you put a drop of soap on the surface? Make sure you save your water strider before it drowns!

Whirligigs

Whirligig beetles are named for the swirling way they swim on the water's surface. Their gyrating motion is where their family name (Gyrinidae) comes from.

Whirligigs have four eyes! Their compound eyes are divided so that the top half sees above water and the lower half sees underwater. Whirligigs are predators that use their raptorial front legs to catch and hold prey.

Have Fun with Chemical Locomotion

Remember the way soap affects the surface tension of water? Whirligigs may be using chemicals this way to help them swim. Try this fun experiment to check it out.

What you need

10-cm (4 inch) square of aluminum foil
Safety pin or sewing needle
Dish soap
Small tub or bucket

What to do

1 Press the foil into the palm of your hand. Fold up your hand and make a small cup from the foil.

2 Punch a tiny hole at the bottom of one side of the cup with the tip of the safety pin or needle.

3 Gently place the cup so that it floats on some water in a small tub. Add a small drop of dish soap in the cup near the hole you punched. What happens? Why?

Mayfly subimagos leaving water

The subimagos leave the water and fly to safety, where they molt to their adult form. Adults may only live for a few hours. They do not eat and do not have mouthparts. Mayflies often leave the water only a few days of the year. Leaving the water at the same time helps them find mates and lowers the chance a predator will catch any one mayfly.

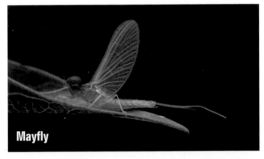

Mayfly

Streams

Streams are fun places to go collecting because many of the insects living there look very different from insects you see in other places. Be on the lookout for juvenile mayflies, stoneflies, caddisflies, and dobsonflies.

Mayfly naiad

Stonefly naiad

Mayflies

You may find large numbers of mayflies in one place. They only feed as naiads. Some species are predators, while others are filter feeders or algae eaters. Some species have fossorial front legs to help them burrow into streambeds. Mayflies are unique because they go through a winged sub-adult stage called a subimago.

Stoneflies

Stonefly naiads look a lot like mayflies. To tell them apart, look for two cerci "tails," two tarsal claws, and gills on the thorax. Some stoneflies called shredders are important in headwater streams because they tear up large leaves, breaking them down into smaller bits of organic matter that can be used by other organisms.

Caddisflies

Caddisfly larvae have a C-shape and a pair of single hooks at the tip of their abdomen. Unlike mayflies and stoneflies, they go through a pupal stage before becoming adults. Caddisflies pupate underwater!

Some caddisflies are free-living predators and some live in cases that they build from silk glands in their mouths. The case homes may have a silken net that filters food from the water.

Other caddisflies build cases from things they find in streams. Some species use grains of sand or small pebbles to build their cases. Others use sticks or bits of leaves. These caddisflies carry their cases with them. The cases help protect them from predators and keep them from being washed downstream by currents.

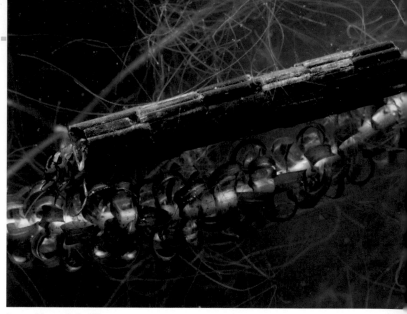

Log cabin case builder

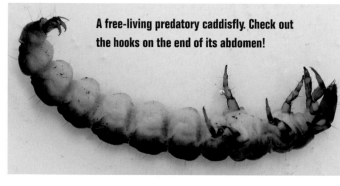

A free-living predatory caddisfly. Check out the hooks on the end of its abdomen!

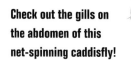

Check out the gills on the abdomen of this net-spinning caddisfly!

Have Fun Watching
Caddisflies Build Cases

It's fun to watch caddisflies build their cases. Some people have used caddisflies to make jewelry by giving them grains of gold and silver!

What you need

Caddisfly larva in its case
Water and plant material from where you collect the larva
Small aquarium
Aquarium aeration pump
Small bowl

What to do

1 Remove the larva from the tank and place it in a small bowl. Carefully remove the larva's case with your fingertips.

2 Place the larva back in the tank and place its case materials near it. How long does it take before the larva starts building a new case?

	Mayflies Ephemeroptera	**Stoneflies** Plecoptera	**Caddisflies** Trichoptera
"Tails"	3 (formed by two cerci and a middle filament)	2 (formed by cerci)	Single hooks
Claws	Single claws on the tips of their legs	Double claws on the tips of their legs	Single claws on the tips of their legs
Gills	On abdomen	On thorax	On abdomen

Left to right: A caddisfly pupa, a larva removed from its case, and a larva in its gravel case

3 Repeat Step 1 and place the larva back in the tank. Instead of giving the larva its original case materials, try giving it something else — small seed beads? Small twigs or leaves? Glitter? Your results will depend on the caddisfly species you collected and the type of case it uses in the wild.

HEALTHY Streams

Scientists look for juvenile mayflies, stoneflies, dobsonflies, and caddisflies to learn about stream ecosystems. These insects do not do well in polluted streams or in streams that do not have the right pH or the right amount of oxygen.

Hellgrammites

Hellgrammites are the larval stage of dobsonflies. Their body and jaw sizes are amazing. These ferocious predators of aquatic insects have sets of fleshy gills along their abdomens and two pairs of hooks at the ends of their abdomens. These sabertoothed insects can reach 7.5 cm (3 inches) in length! Aren't you glad you're not a mayfly or a stonefly? In some species, adult males have extra-large mandibles that they use to fight other males.

Plants

Many, many species of insects can be found on all kinds of plants: grasses, green leafy and flowering plants, garden vegetables and flowers, shrubs, and trees. You might imagine that you would find different insects on an oak tree than you would on garden vegetables. The tree and the garden each have their own communities. A community includes all the living organisms in that place. Think of it like a biological neighborhood that can be big or small.

For example, on a single tree, you can find insects that feed on the tree (herbivores), insects that scavenge waste and debris (scavengers), and insects that prey on other insects (predators). You may also find insects that parasitize other insects (parasites), and insects that are just pausing for a while on the tree for shelter or a place to warm up.

Living on Plants

What do you think living on a plant is like? What would you eat? Where would you rest? Is there anywhere to hide from predators? Insects that live on plants find cool solutions to these challenges.

SHELTER

Insects living on plants need shelter from predators and parasites, and also from sun and wind. Unlike insects that live in ponds, streams, and leaf litter, insects on plants are exposed to the sun and air. It's easy for them to lose too much water and dry out. If you don't see any insects when you first look at a plant, think about where on the plant an insect would be sheltered from the

Above: Ladybugs in wood crevices

Above: Spittle bug shelter; below: Gall wasp and gall larva

sun and wind. For example, look on the undersides of leaves or branches.

Some insects make shelters for themselves by rolling up leaves, or with webbing or debris. Froghopper nymphs called spittlebugs make shelter from bubbly foam. When they blow air out of spiracles near their butts, the air mixes with plant sap that the nymph releases . . . this is the foam you see!

Other insects find shelter by living inside the plant's living tissues. For example, tiny wasps lay eggs in the leaves and twigs of oak trees. As the eggs hatch and the wasp larvae begin to feed, this small part of the plant grows into a gall, or a protective shell made of plant tissue. After the wasp larvae become adults and leave the gall, other insects and arthropods sometimes move in!

FOOD

Eating plants is called herbivory (er-BIV-er-ee), and animals that eat plants are herbivores. There are several different ways to be an herbivore.

Some insects are specialists: they eat only one kind of plant. For example, in the upland prairie of western Oregon, female Fender's blue butterflies lay their eggs on a flowering plant called Kincaid's lupine, and Fender's blue caterpillars depend on Kincaid's lupine for food.

Some insects specialize on a group of related plants. For example, monarchs eat different species of plants in the milkweed family.

Other insects are generalists and can eat many kinds of plants. Most grasshoppers, crickets, and katydids are generalists.

Many kinds of female insects lay their eggs on plants so their nymphs or larvae will be near the right food. You may also find pupae on plants.

Butterfly eggs

FIGHTING PLANT DEFENSES

Plants stick up for themselves! Many plants use toxins to defend themselves from herbivores. Others use thorns, spines, prickly hairs, and thick waxy coatings to protect themselves. Some plants even release odors that attract predators and parasitoids when insects start feeding on them.

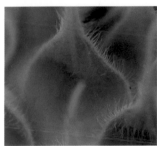

Ants & Plants

Ants move a lot of seeds around, and they even plant them! Some plants make seeds decorated with small packets of food to attract ants. Ant workers bring these seed packets back to their nests and feed the food part of the packets to their larvae. Some of the leftover seeds grow into plants.

Ant food on seed

Many plants are defended by ants! Some plants have hollow stems or thorns that ants use as shelters. Other plants make special food rewards for their ants, but these rewards are on the plants themselves, not on the seeds. Ants that live on plants with shelters or food rewards defend their plant from all kinds of herbivores, even from large vertebrates.

Bug Camp Activity

Look carefully at the leaves of plants outside. Look at the edges, tops, and bottoms of the leaves. Can you tell which kinds of insects have been feeding on your plants?

Chewers use mandibles to chew leaves and other plant tissues. If you see this type of leaf damage, it might be caused by orthopterans, stick insects, caterpillars, beetles, or hymenopterans.

Look for chewing damage on the edges or middles of leaves.

Miners feed inside a leaf. They eat cells that are in between the top and bottom surfaces of leaves. Sometimes, if you hold up a mined leaf, you can see frass in the mine, too. (Frass is the name for insect poop!) If you find a leaf mine, it was probably caused by a larva of Coleoptera, Diptera, Lepidoptera, or Hymenoptera (sawflies).

Leaf mines

Feeding on plant juices with piercing mouthparts

Sap-suckers punch into plant vessels with their piercing-sucking mouthparts. (Did you know that plants have vessels to move things around, just like you have arteries and veins?) Plant damage from sap-suckers can be harder to see than damage from chewers and miners. Many hemipterans feed this way.

When you look at leaves and branches, you may also find galls. Galls are made by wasps and some kinds of aphids and thrips.

Galls can be big or small.

Science at Work

Plants often defend themselves with chemicals against caterpillars. Researchers found that plants make more anti-caterpillar chemicals after being chewed on. That's pretty cool — the plant responds to being eaten by the caterpillar and defends itself.

Think about: How do you know when a person or animal is near you? You hear, smell, or see them. Two researchers named Heidi and Rex realized that when a caterpillar chews on a plant, it produces vibrations. They wondered if plants would make chemicals in response to just the vibrations, without being chewed on.

Rex Cocroft and Heidi Appel shook a single leaf on a plant exactly the same way that a chewing caterpillar does. The gentle shaking caused the plant to defend its other leaves. They did this work with a lot of plants. The plants defended themselves in response to the vibrations of chewing caterpillars. Researchers still don't know how plants *sense* the vibrations. Maybe they will by the time you read this book!

FECES
(dung & poop)

From a human point of view, feces can be gross. For animals, it's a high-energy food, and many kinds of insects use animal poop for food for themselves or their young. Without dung-eating insects, everyone would be knee-deep in poop! Insects that eat feces face two big problems. First, it's not always easy to find. Second, it dries out quickly and may not be edible for long. These two problems mean there is a lot of competition for fresh feces.

A fun way to find unusual insects is to look at poop. At a farm, try looking for insects that live in the poop under a chicken coop. Or flip over cow pies in a cow pasture. You may find adult and larval flies, dermestid beetles, and adult and larval dung beetles. The types of insects you will find can depend on how moist the cow pie is. Wear rubber gloves when you search in this habitat!

Dung beetles are probably the most spectacular insects you can find in feces. They come in many sizes, shapes, and colors. Some are beautiful metallic reds, greens, and golds, and they often have large horns

for fighting. These beetles can use all types of dung, but they mostly use poop from herbivores. Some dung beetles are only found in the dung of one kind of animal.

Although dung has some undigested food in it, most dung beetles may be eating the many micro-organisms that live in dung liquid. Dung beetles even have special mouthparts for slurping up this yummy — well, yummy to them, anyway — liquid. Dung beetles also use dung to feed and rear their young. There are three types of dung beetles, and the types are decided by how the beetles behave at dung piles.

Type 1: Dwellers

Dwellers feed or lay eggs right on the dung pile. Larvae grow up in the dung, and can still use dung after it's dried out. The next two types of dung beetles need fresh, moist dung. They keep dung moist by burying it.

Type 2: Rollers

Rollers scoop out small piles of dung, make balls from them, and roll the dung balls away from the dung pile. Two types of balls are formed by these tumblebugs. One type is for eating, and both males and females make these balls. The other type is for rearing young, and is called a brood ball. Males make these dung balls to attract females for mating.

Once a male/female pair forms, they roll the ball away from the pile and bury it in soft soil. The pair mates and the female lays an egg in the brood ball. Depending on the species, the female may stay to care for the growing larvae. Males leave to find another dung pile and another mate. Rollers tend to have scooped heads for shaping dung balls and large fossorial front legs for burying balls.

Think about it. Why do you think rollers move their dung balls away from the pile? Sometimes, other beetles challenge a roller and try to steal its dung ball!

Type 3: Tunnelers

Tunnelers burrow through dung piles until they hit the soil below, where both males and females make burrows. Because the burrows are just under the dung pile, young beetles have a large supply of fresh dung. Males and females also work together to dig

small rooms off the main burrow called brood chambers. They fill these chambers with fresh dung, and then females lay eggs on the dung. Males stand guard at the entrance to the tunnel to keep out other males, predators, and parasites. Guarding males have specialized horns that help them fight off enemies.

Have Fun
Testing Beetle Strength

Male dung beetles are extremely strong and can push rival beetles from their tunnel's entrance. One species of tunneling dung beetle has been dubbed the strongest animal on the planet because it can pull more than 1,000 times its body weight!

What you need

Beetle or other insect
25-cm (10 inch) length of dental floss
Short length of wood with a groove
    about 1.5 times as wide as the beetle

Small plastic cup
Small fishing weights
Nail
Small scale

What to do

1 To prepare the beetle, tie a length of dental floss around its middle, between the prothorax and abdomen. Leave one end of the dental floss trailing behind the beetle.

2 To prepare the cup, punch a hole just below the rim with the tip of the nail. Tie the trailing end of the dental floss through the cup. Your cup should now be attached to the beetle.

3 Lay the piece of wood on the edge of a table with the grooved surface facing up. Place the beetle in the groove facing away from the edge of the table. Dangle the cup off the edge of the wood (and the table). Add some weight to the cup to find out how much the beetle can lift. Measure the weight of the beetle and the cup. Can you figure out how much weight you would need to lift to match the beetle?

Rearing & Keeping
LIVE INSECTS

It is amazing to just sit and watch insects. Even when you keep them indoors, some insects behave just as they do in the wild. Most insects do well inside if you give them the right food, temperature, and water. Below are a few insects that are easy to rear and keep in home labs. If you decide to keep other insects, be sure to identify them so you can find out what kind of food and habitat they need.

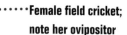

Female field cricket; note her ovipositor

Field Crickets

Field crickets are very easy to keep inside. You will need a small cage or plastic container about the size of a shoebox to house them. If you use a cage, choose one with fine wire mesh. (Some crickets can chew through plastic screens and small hatchlings can escape through larger mesh.) Make sure there are no cracks along the edges. A container that easily opens from the top works best.

To collect field crickets, look under logs, boards, or rocks in a field. Adults have tegmina. Males and females are easy to tell apart. Females have a sharp needle-like ovipositor sticking out from the tip of their abdomen.

If you find males and females, put several into your container and watch what happens. Males may make chirps or trills, depending on their species. Watch how they make the sound by moving their wings. When they are alone, males make a loud calling song. When they are near a female, males make a quieter, courtship sound. If another male is close by, they make a shrill, aggressive sound. How many types of songs can you hear?

Male field cricket

Have Fun Experimenting with Circadian Rhythms in Crickets

Feed your crickets small pieces of apple, carrot, lettuce, and a few small pieces of dry cat or dog chow. If you have sand or soil in your cage, the food may get moldy. Remove any moldy food and replace it with fresh food every other day.

You can watch females lay eggs in sandy soil by placing a small glass dish in the cage with about 5 cm (2 inches) of moist sand. Take the dish out every few days and look for eggs along the side of the glass. Keep the sand moist and in a few weeks you will have very small crickets hatching! Crickets have simple metamorphosis and look like tiny adults when they hatch from eggs. Feed them the same foods you feed the adults.

Field cricket eggs in moist sand

Crickets are nocturnal animals so most of their activity occurs at night. Crickets and most other nocturnal animals can be "clock shifted" so that they become active during the day. You can even get them to chirp during the day.

To clock shift crickets, you will need a room or container with a light that can be turned off and on at specific times of the day. Get a simple light timer at your local hardware or building supply store and set the clock so the light comes on during the night and goes off during the day.

The day length is called the photoperiod, and changes with season and latitude. To mimic summertime, for example, you will need to have the lights on for longer than you have them off. If you live around 20° to 40° latitude, it's probably fourteen hours of light and ten hours of dark. Because most insects cannot see red, you can watch them with a red light while the other light is off. The crickets will still think it is dark!

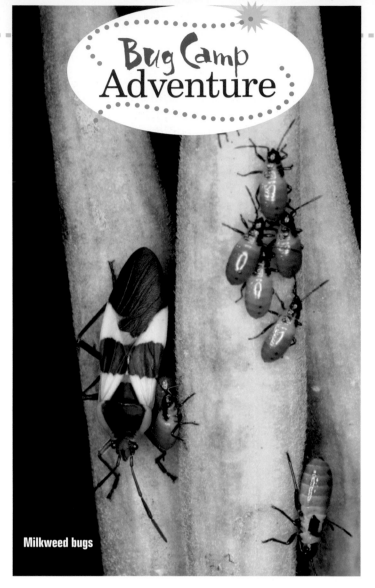

Bug Camp
Adventure

Milkweed Bugs

Milkweed bugs are easy to collect and to keep at home. Look for them on milkweed plants during the summer and early fall. Milkweed is named for the white sap that oozes from cuts in the plant. The sap is poisonous so do not put the plants or the insects in your mouth and always wash your hands after working with them. Can you guess why most of the insects that live on milkweeds have bright red, orange, and black colors?

Milkweed bugs feed on the milkweed seeds so they are often on the seedpods. To collect and rear them, a wide-mouthed Mason jar works well. Remove the lid and hold a piece of cloth or screen over the top with a rubber band. Place sticks, milkweed, or paper towels in the jar so your insects have places to crawl and hide. Feed them sunflower (raw or unsalted), squash, watermelon, or almond seeds. Clean your cages by removing any frass and dried seeds. Add water every other day with a light misting from a spray bottle.

Milkweed bug nymphs hatch from eggs. The nymphs look and act like adults without wings, and molt several times as they grow. Watch for wing buds right before they molt into adults.

Milkweed bugs

Butterflies

Can you name the stages of a butterfly lifecycle? The cycle begins with an egg laid by a female. Eggs are usually laid on or near the plant that the caterpillar will eat. (When you were looking for milkweed bugs, you may have seen monarch butterfly caterpillars because they feed on milkweed, too.) To grow larger, caterpillars have to molt and shed their skin. When they get big enough, they molt into a pupa or chrysalis. Finally, the adult emerges from the pupa. All butterflies go through similar stages: egg, larva, pupa, and adult. This kind of lifecycle is called complete metamorphosis. With complete metamorphosis, the larvae and adults eat different

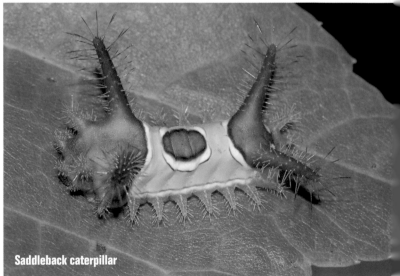

Saddleback caterpillar

foods and live in different habitats. Larvae and adults also have adaptations that help them do different jobs. The caterpillar's job is to eat and avoid being seen and eaten by predators. The adult's job is to fly, reproduce, and find new places to live. You can watch this amazing transformation right in your home lab. All you need is a good cage and some food. (A good cage is easy to open, clean, and add things for the caterpillar to climb and feed on.)

If you find a caterpillar feeding in the wild, collect both the caterpillar and a few leaves from the plant. Be careful when handling caterpillars because some species have spines and hairs that can irritate your skin. Caterpillars eat a lot so you may need to return to the plant where you found it (or another one of the same kind) to cut a few fresh leaves every day for your caterpillar's food. If you find the caterpillar in a garden, check with the garden's owner before cutting up their plants!

When caterpillars are ready to molt, they stop eating and moving for a few days. They shed their skin, pushing the old skin off of the end of their abdomen. When caterpillars are large

Swallowtail LIFECYCLE

enough and ready to pupate, they stop eating and go into a "wandering" stage when they will walk around and around their cage. They may lose water during this stage so it's a good idea to add a few paper towels to the cage to absorb it.

Yellow bear caterpillar

Monarch caterpillar over time, shedding and molting into a pupa

Map butterfly lifecycle

Depending on the caterpillar, they may form a chrysalis or they may spin a cocoon. Add some sticks in the cage so the caterpillar can pupate hanging down. If your caterpillar species normally pupates in the soil, they may pupate on the floor of your cage. Remember that adults need space to let their wings expand and dry after pupating.

Hickory-horned devil

Bug Camp
Experiment

Have Fun Measuring Caterpillar Growth

Caterpillars are eating machines. It seems like that is all they do: eat, eat, and eat some more! You can chart the growth by measuring a caterpillar's length or weight every day and recording the data in your notebook. Because caterpillar bodies are flexible, it might be better to measure a hard part such as the width of their head. If you collect the shed skin, you can measure the width of the head capsule using your digital phone microscope. Make sure you take the photos at the same distance and with a ruler in the shot.

Still curious? If you have a sensitive scale you can estimate how good caterpillars are at digesting their food. Every day, weigh these four things: your caterpillar, the food left over from the day before, the fresh food you added, and the frass in the bottom of the cage. Write down your data in a notebook. A sample notebook page is below. You might predict that the amount of weight gained should equal the amount of food eaten minus the weight of the frass produced. Does your prediction hold? If not, why do you think it's different?

	Day 1	Day 2	Day 3
Weight of Caterpillar			
Weight of Leftover Food			
Weight of New Food			
Weight of Frass in Bottom of Cage			

Mosquito larvae breathing through siphons

Mosquitoes

Chances are that you are already rearing mosquitoes around your house. All of the juvenile stages live in water and can grow up in any small puddle of water. Check in tree holes, birdbaths, or any other small pool of standing water near your house.

You can create a habitat for mosquitoes by putting out small containers filled with water. (Black containers work best.) If you add some crushed leaves and a few flakes of rabbit, fish, or guinea pig food, mosquitoes will colonize the water faster. Soon, female mosquitoes will lay eggs on or near the water. Check with your parents because they may not want mosquitoes growing up around their house!

Larvae that hatch from eggs have a large head and thorax, and look very different from winged adults. You can bring some larvae and water into your home lab and keep them in a plastic container or small aquarium. Make sure you have a tight-fitting lid on the container or aquarium so the emerging adults do not escape into your house.

To get air, larvae place a snorkel-like body part

Mosquito Life Cycle

Adult mosquito

Eggs (in egg raft)

Larva (wriggler)

Pupa

called a siphon that's at the tip of their abdomen at the water's surface. Disturb them and use a magnifying glass to watch how they swim. Why do you think they are called wigglers? Keep watching.

WHAT HAPPENS NEXT?
Look for the brushy mouthparts on the larvae that help them eat algae. As they feed, they grow and molt several times into larger and larger larvae. When the larvae get big enough, they molt to the pupal stage. Pupae also need to come to the water surface to breathe, but they uses two "horns" on their thorax as snorkels. You can watch the adult taking shape inside the pupa. Adults break out of their pupal skin at the water's surface and fly away.

At this stage, females need to mate with a male and feed on blood before they can lay eggs. Only females bite! Mosquito larvae and adults are very different from each other. Larvae are adapted for living in water and eating algae, while adults are adapted for flying, feeding on blood, and reproducing. Mosquitoes have a pupal stage so their lifecycle is more complex than the lifecycles of crickets and milkweed bugs.

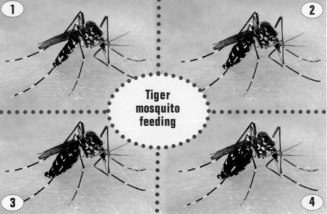

1

2

Tiger mosquito feeding

3

4

41

COLLECTING

Luckily, insects are just about everywhere, making them very easy to find, watch, and collect. The following are some places and techniques you can use to find and collect insects of all sorts. Have fun!

HAND Picking

One of the easiest ways to collect insects is to use a small vial or plastic jar to capture them by hand. Clear vials or jars let you watch the insect and examine it up close. You never know when you may encounter a cool and interesting insect, so it is a great idea to carry at least a few small vials in your pocket or backpack.

To catch an insect, hold the lid in one hand and the vial in the other and carefully close the insect inside. Make sure not to pinch the insect's wings or legs when you close the lid. Some of the best places for hand-picking are on flowers. Go out to the nearest patch of flowers and see what you find!

Swooping and sweeping can help you bag some interesting specimens.

NETS

There are many types of nets for collecting insects.

AERIAL NETS are made of light netting material so that the weight of the net bag does not damage the insects when they are caught. Aerial nets are good for catching flying insects such as butterflies.

One technique for an aerial net is to swing the net to capture the insect in the net's bag. At the end of your swing, flip the net to close the opening so that the insect is trapped in the net and cannot escape. It takes some practice to learn to make the swing and flip moves all in one motion.

Because many flying insects will fly upward as an escape response, another technique is to bring the net down over the insects and hold the tip of the bag up. Usually, insects will climb or fly up to the top of the net.

SWEEP NETS are a great way to collect a wide variety of insects in tall grass and bushes.

Because the nets need to withstand briars, sharp branches, sticks, and grass blades, sweep nets are made of muslin material that is thicker than the aerial netting.

The sweep net technique is simple. While walking through grass or bushes, sweep the net back and forth in front of your legs. The motion will knock insects off the plants and into the net. Just like the aerial net, on your last sweep flip the net to close the bag to keep the insects from escaping.

Use a kick net to catch aquatic insects.

Dip nets are easy to use.

KICK NETS and **DIP NETS** are used to collect insects that live in or near water. To collect insects in streams, place the open end of the kick net so it faces upstream. Kick and brush the rocks in front of the net. The flow of the moving water will wash nearby aquatic insects into the net.

To collect insects in the weeds along the shore of a pond or lake, use a dip net to scoop up insects. If you do not have a dip net or kick net, a kitchen strainer will work well — just make sure you wash it before using it to strain spaghetti!

TRAPS

Entomologists use several types of traps for collecting insects.

PITFALL TRAPS are a great way to catch crawling insects. You can easily build this type of trap. Bury an empty cup in the ground so that the lip of the cup is at ground level. Make a small tent over the cup with wood, plastic, or stones to keep rain from filling the cup. To increase your catch, you can add bait such as peanut butter, dung, cat food, or other stinky foods. You can also place a funnel in the top of the cup to keep flying insects from escaping.

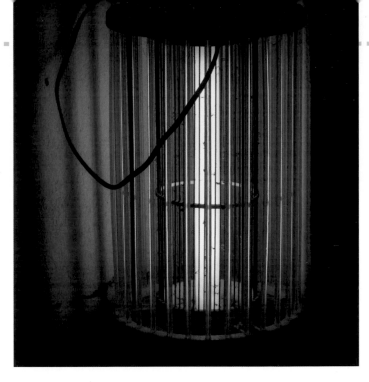

A cup inside a cup makes it easy to check and remove the insects in your pitfall trap.

LIGHT TRAPS are a fun way to collect night-flying insects. If you have ever noticed the way insects are attracted to porch lights at night then you have already seen these traps at work. One of the best lights for attracting insects is a blacklight. These lights emit ultraviolet light that insects can see and will move toward. This is why blacklights are used in BUG ZAPPERS!

You may want to place a large white bedsheet in front of your porch light or a blacklight. The sheet makes the lighted area larger and it's easy to see and capture the insects that land on it. This is a great way to collect antlions, moths, and beetles. If you place a light trap near a water source, you can attract mayflies, stoneflies, caddisflies, and dobsonflies.

Berlese Funnels

These funnels allow you to collect small insects and other animals found in soil and leaf litter. To use a Berlese funnel, place a small piece of wire mesh or cheesecloth in the bottom of the funnel. Place a handful of moist leaf litter and soil in the funnel, and then place the funnel over a jar filled with alcohol.

Be green! Re-use your two-liter plastic bottles to make funnels.

Place the funnel in a window or below a lamp. As the heat from the sun or lamp dries the leaf litter, the animals will move deeper into the litter until they fall through the funnel and into the jar.

Transferring to Vials

What do you do after you have caught an insect in a net or trap? You transfer it to a vial!

To transfer insects from a net, hold the closed end of the net facing upward so that the insect climbs to the top. Use one hand to grasp around the net to keep the insect trapped. Then, take a vial (without a lid) in your other hand and move it into the net, trapping the insect in the vial against the net. Put the lid on.

To transfer insects from a light or pitfall trap, move a vial (without a lid) under an insect. With your other hand, bring the lid down as you scoop the vial upward.

Pooters

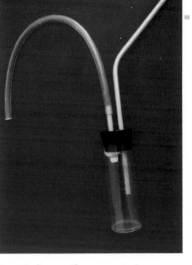

A pooter, or aspirator, is a fun, efficient tool for "vacuuming" up tiny insects. It is simply two tubes that are glued into a container or that go through a stopper in a vial. You suck on one tube and use the other tube to vacuum the insect into the vial or other container. Once you have made a pooter, you can use it to pick up very small insects in sweep nets and on plants. In case you were wondering, the pooter was named for an entomologist, Frederick Poos.

To use a pooter, place the sucking tube in your mouth and the other near an insect. Suck on the tube and the insect will end up in your vial! Have a contest with your friends to see who can collect the most insects with a pooter. Because you are sucking in air, it is also a good idea to look at what you might be getting into your lungs. Never use a pooter near feces or carrion, for example. Some entomologists put a small electric vacuum on the sucking tube.

Have Fun Making & Using a Pooter!

What you need

Plastic vial
Rubber stopper with two holes
   5-mm (3/16 inch) diameter
Two 10-cm (4 inch) lengths plastic tubing
   or two bendable drinking straws
Waterproof marker
2.5-cm (1 inch) square of fine plastic screen
   mesh or muslin fabric
Rubber band or tape
25-cm (10 inch) length of rubber tubing, optional

What to do

1 Double check that your stopper will fit into your vial and that your straws or plastic tubing will fit into the stopper holes.

2 Remove the stopper from the vial and insert about 2 inches of each straw or piece of tubing into the stopper. You may need to squeeze the straws closed to get them into the holes.

3 Choose one of the straws or pieces of tubing to be the one you will suck on. Label it near the top with a dot or the letter S with a marker. Label the other tubing near the top with the letter B for Bug.

4 Place the bottom of the sucking tube in the center of the screen or muslin. Fold the screen up against the straw and hold it in place with a rubber band or tape. **Important:** Do a good job with this step. The screen will work like a filter, keeping insects from being sucked into your mouth!

5 Place the stopper back in the vial. Have fun sucking up insects!

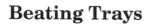

Beating Trays

To collect insects in bushes or that live on tree branches, bug campers and scientists use beating trays. Any white pan or plastic tub will work. Place the pan or tub under a tree branch. Hit the branch with a stick hard enough to jar the insects from the branch so they fall into the pan or tub. Use a vial or pooter to collect them.

Notebooks

Scientists keep their information and observations (data) in notebooks or store them in files on computers. A notebook is a handy way to record information in the field and to keep track of when and where you collected particular specimens. Once you collect a specimen, you will want to record three important pieces of information:

1 Where you collected the insect

2 The date you found the insect

3 Your name as the collector

Other information you might want to include in your notebook is general information on weather, how you collected the insect, a sketch of the insect, and a description of what it was doing when you found it.

Above: Sometimes you have to beat the bushes to get insects.

Bug Camper
Safety Tips

• Always let someone know when and where you're going collecting.

• If you're collecting aquatic insects, wear water-safe shoes with good soles. Never collect insects from a fast-moving stream that's higher than your knees.

• If you collect insects from dead animals or feces, be sure to wear gloves and wash your hands well afterward.

• Be very careful to watch for cars if you go collecting near roads.

INSECTS in
COLLECTIONS

Have you ever been to a natural history museum? They are great places to see many different types of animals and plants. What have you seen in museums? Dinosaurs? Lions and tigers? Crocodiles or whales? Besides being fun adventures for visitors, museums have an important scientific purpose. They are full of data — the details about what, when, how, and where their organisms were found. This information helps scientists know where animals are found around the world. Keeping track of these details over time can help scientists understand how our world is changing.

In addition to the large animals above, most museums also have collections of insects and other small animals. You can make and keep insect collections, too. You just need to learn how to preserve your insects, how to label them, and how to care for a collection so it can be useful to science.

Killing Insects

It is great fun to watch living insects, but to make a collection, insects need to be killed and preserved. Before you begin, it's always a good idea to learn about your local species so you don't collect any that might be endangered or threatened. Also, when you can, collect males instead of females so you will have less impact on local insects. Not all males and females look different in the same insect group, but in some groups it's easy to tell males from females because females have ovipositors at the ends of their bodies.

KILL JARS

Kill jars are one way to kill insects. You can find them in nature stores and online. Ask an adult to help you add a small amount of a poison in a cotton ball that will quickly kill your specimens. Fingernail polish remover (acetone) is often used.

If you use acetone, try not to use too much because the liquid acetone may get on your insects and discolor them. To use a kill jar, open it quickly, put the insects in, and close the jar before they escape. Make sure your insects are dead before you begin to pin and mount them. Keeping them in a kill jar overnight works well.

Safety notes: Never breathe the fumes in a kill jar. Ask an adult to help you find a safe place to store your kill jar so younger kids will not think it's a toy and play with it.

FREEZING

Freezing is another way to kill insects. Because their body temperatures are the same as the outside temperature, insects placed in a kitchen freezer become less and less active as they freeze. Some insects can handle freezing so make sure that they are dead before you begin pinning them! Let them thaw completely before you pin them.

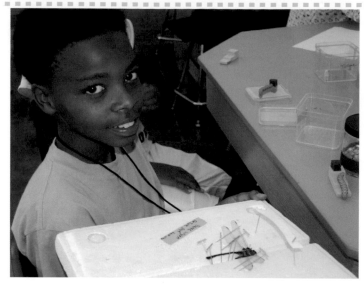

PINNING & Mounting Insects

Most large, adult insects are suitable for pinning. Some soft-bodied insects such as mayflies and termites are better kept in small vials of alcohol. It is always best to pin an insect that is fresh and has not dried out. Once they dry out, they are brittle and easily broken. Entomologists use special pins to mount their insects. The pins come in different sizes to match the different sizes of insects. Most insects can be pinned using #1 or #2 insect pins.

Bug Camper Tip

It is always good practice to keep the collecting information with your specimens. A small piece of tape with the place, date, and collector information makes a good temporary label.

Placing Pins

The first step to pinning an insect is deciding where the pin should go. Look at the pinning places shown with red dots in the figures. Notice that the pins go in the thorax and, in most cases, to the right of the midline. Pins usually go to one side of the midline because the pin will destroy a

Stick with These Pinning Locations

Bees, wasps, and flies: between forewings to right of midline

Beetles: upper left of right elytra

Butterflies & moths: see pages 52 & 53

Dragonflies: to right of midline at base of forewings

Grasshoppers and crickets: right of the middle line through prothorax

True bugs: in triangle to right of midline

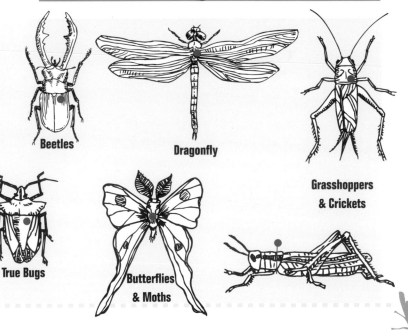

Bees, Wasps & Flies

Beetles

Dragonfly

Grasshoppers & Crickets

True Bugs

Butterflies & Moths

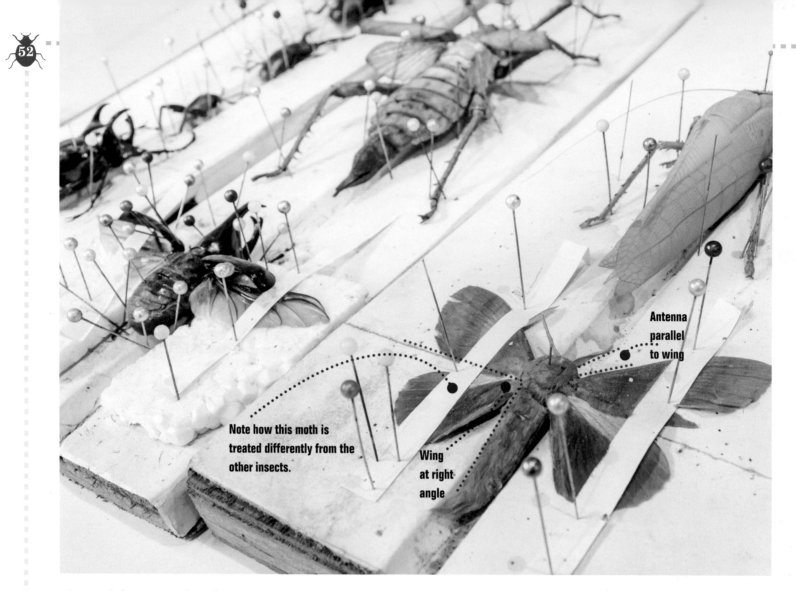

Note how this moth is treated differently from the other insects.

Wing at right angle

Antenna parallel to wing

piece of the animal and you may need that piece later to identify the insect. Because the left and right halves of an insect are the same, you can look at the other half to see what is missing where the pin is!

To pin an insect, hold it between your thumb and forefinger. Using your other hand, stick the pin just through the top of the insect at the correct position. Try to keep the pin straight up and down with respect to the insect body. Once you have the pin straight, push it the rest of the way through.

Next, you need to get the insect at the proper height on the pin. Entomologists use a pinning

block for this step because they keep all of the insects in their collection at the same height on the pins. Pinning blocks can be found at nature stores and online, or you can make your own. Stick the point of the pin in the first (deepest) hole of a pinning block and push the pin through the insect until its point hits the bottom of the hole. If you have a very thick insect, you may need to pull the pin out so that you have something to hold.

Use cardboard or foam blocks to position the legs and wings. Push the pin into the cardboard or foam until the insect just sits on the surface. Now use other pins to move and hold the legs and wings in place.

Butterflies and moths are treated a little differently than most other insects. First, the pin goes right in the middle of the thorax, not to the right. Second, the wings are arranged using a spreading board. To pin a butterfly or moth, push the pin into the groove of the spreading board so that the insect's abdomen is in the groove. Arrange the wings so the hind edge of each front wing is at a right angle to the insect's body. Cut several small strips of paper and place them over the wings. (See photo.) Pin the wings in place by pinning through the paper. Be careful not to put the pins through the wings! Finally, arrange the antennae so they run parallel to the front edge of the wings.

Preserving Insects

Once you have positioned your insects the way you want them to look, you need to preserve them. This step is very easy because insects do it all on their own. Remember that insects have an exoskeleton made from chitin, which is very strong and lasts a long time. To preserve an insect, you just have to let it dry. Drying time depends on the humidity and size of your insect. It can take a few days to a week. Once your insect

is dry, any small bump or touch can cause legs, wings, and antennae to break. By carefully picking them up by their pins, preserved insects will stay in one piece and last for many years.

Labeling Insects

Collectors use insect labels to keep the collecting and identification information with their insects. This information is typed or written in very small lettering on paper and pinned just below the insect. Use sturdy, unlined white paper for labels. Each label should be about 15 x 7 mm (.6 x .3 inches).

THE FIRST LABEL

Details about the collection site go on the first label. This information includes the country, state, county, latitude, longitude, collecting date, and the collector's name. Use this format to show the date, month, and year: 10 Oct 2016. The abbreviation *col* stands for collector.

> USA: FL: Alachua Co.
> Gainesville 29.652N 82.325W
> 10 Oct 2016 col: JE Lloyd

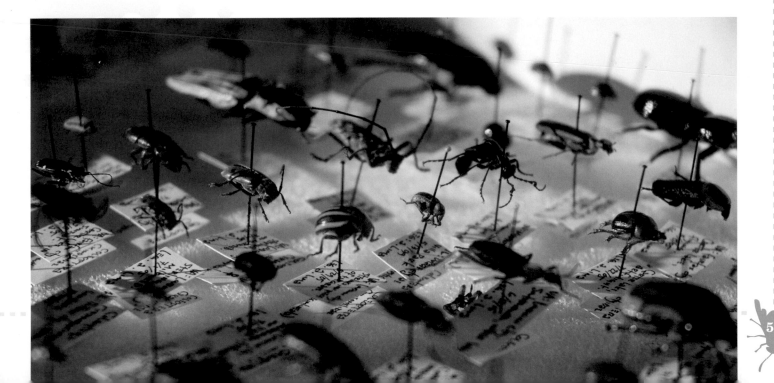

There are many options for displaying your insect collections.

Bug Camp Adventure

Have Fun Making a Pinning Block

You can make your own pinning block with a small piece of wood that is 80 x 40 x 20 mm (3 x 1.5 x ¾ inches). Ask an adult to help you drill three holes with a 1.6-mm (¹⁄₁₆ inch) bit at the following depths: 25 mm (1 inch), 18 mm (¾ inch), and 12 mm (½ inch). Use a waterproof marker to label the holes 1, 2, and 3. The deepest hole (#1) is for pinning the insects. The middle hole (#2) is for positioning the first label on the pin, under the insect. The shallowest hole (#3) is for positioning the second label.

You may need to arrange the information so that it fits neatly on the label. Place the label so that it can be read from the head to the abdomen of the insect and so the bottom of the label is on the animal's left. Push the pin through the middle of the label and put the point in the second hole of the pinning block. Push the pin through the label until it hits the bottom of the pinning block. If you have a thick insect, be extra careful because you do not want to push the label up and break your insect.

THE SECOND LABEL

Identification information goes on the second label. It may include identification details about the animal such as the taxa down to the species, if known. The second label also may include notes on collecting information or habitat, and the person who identified the insect. The abbreviation *det* stands for determined by.

> ORTHOPTERA Tettigoniidae
>
> *Amblycorypha alexanderi*
>
> on *Smilax* det: TJ Walker

Now you are ready to add the final label to your pin. Orient the label to read like the identification label and push the pin through the middle of the label. Put the point in the third hole of the pinning block. Push the pin through the label until it hits the bottom of the pinning block. Done! Now you have a specimen that is both art and science.

Storing Insects

Insects can be stored in a variety of boxes and cabinets ranging from shoeboxes to wooden cases with glass tops. It is best to have a thin foam base that pins can be pushed through to hold your insects upright.

The insects in your collection can last for many years. However, one of the most important things to look out for is an insect. Carpet beetles eat dead insects and can destroy your collection! For home collections, a fresh mothball can protect your insects. To keep the mothball from rolling around and damaging your insects, ask an adult to help you heat the head of a metal pin and push the hot part of the pin into the mothball. Use pliers to hold the pin so you don't burn your fingers. Replace the mothball every few months.

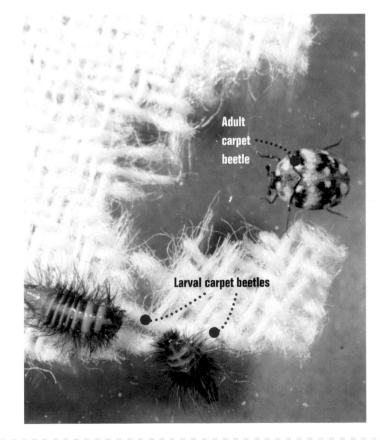

Adult carpet beetle

Larval carpet beetles

PREDATORS

Insects that eat plants, pollen, and nectar can be fun to watch, but far and away the coolest insects to see feeding are the predators. Their adaptations for capturing prey are incredible. After you've watched them for a while, you will be glad they're so small. Imagine if they were the same size as a large dog!

This is a larval antlion. They live in sandpits and eat ants.

ANTLION fun

Have you ever seen small funnels in the dry sand under an eave or bridge? Those are antlion pits! At the bottom of each pit is a hungry larva with very large, sharp jaws.

An antlion pit is a perfect trap. When an ant falls into the pit, the antlion throws sand and knocks the ant back down into the antlion's waiting jaws.

You can capture antlions and bring them home to watch.

Bug Camp Adventure

Catching Antlions

What you need

Antlions
Plastic or metal spoon
Kitchen strainer or sieve
Collection vial(s)
Small plastic tub about 7.5 cm (3 inches) deep
Sand

What to do

1 Find a place where there are lots of antlion pits.

2 Use the spoon to quickly scoop up the bottom of an antlion's pit.

3 Put the scoop of sand in the strainer and gently shake to sift out the sand.

4 The antlions are sometimes camouflaged and may be difficult to see at the bottom of the strainer. Once you find them, put them in a vial.

5 At home, you can have fun watching them build pits and catch prey. Put the antlion on the top of the sand and watch what happens. The antlion will probably burrow into the sand right away. How does it burrow? It may take a little while before the antlion is ready to build a pit. Write down what you observe. How does the antlion move as it throws sand? What body part does it use to throw sand?

Antlions live inside these pits in soft soil and sand.

Bug Camp Experiment

Rearing Antlions

Antlions have complete metamorphosis, just like butterflies. You can rear antlion larvae in your container of sand. Feed an ant to each antlion every day or so. (When they are ready to feed, they will be at the bottom of the pit.) You will notice short periods when they stop feeding. These are the times that they are molting. If you begin with large larvae, you can feed them until they pupate.

If the larvae have not fed for a long while, sift the sand with your strainer and you may find small balls of sand. Antlion larvae use silk to glue grains of sand around them to create a safe place to pupate.

Adult antlions have wings like dragonflies

When the adults emerge from their pupal case, they will need to hang from a stick or screen to let their wings expand and dry.

Antlion larva

WATER SCORPIONS
& Toe Biters!

Two of the most ferocious insects you will find in ponds are water scorpions and giant water bugs. Both have front legs adapted for grasping prey. They also have piercing-sucking mouthparts used to suck the juices from their victims. Giant water bugs are sometimes called toe biters because they bite if people step on them!

Water scorpions and toe biters live in water as both nymphs and adults. They are easy to tell apart. Water scorpions have a long breathing tube called a siphon at the tip of their abdomen. They use it like a snorkel to stay submerged in water. Another difference is that water scorpions move by walking, while giant water bugs use their hind legs to swim.

Water scorpions have a long breathing tube called a siphon that helps them breathe underwater.

This toe biter, a.k.a giant water bug, uses its powerful hind legs for swimming and its front legs for grasping prey.

Below left: water scorpion with visible siphon
Below: giant water bug using piercing mouthparts on fish prey

Have Fun Rearing & Feeding Water Scorpions & Giant Water Bugs

What you need

Small aquarium or plastic container
Small bucket or other waterproof container
Plants and water from the collection site
Food (live insects)
Forceps or tweezers

What to do

1 Catch some water scorpions or giant water bugs with a dipnet around plants near the shorelines of a pond or lake.

2 Fill your bucket or other container with pond or lake water. Add a few stems from plants found near the water.

3 Place the water scorpions or giant water bugs in an aquarium filled about a third of the way with water. Add a few plant stems.

4 Hand-feed your animals by lowering several insects into the water with forceps or tweezers every few days. Place the prey right in front of your animals. Invite your friends and family to watch the hunting fun.

Bug Notes: Be careful what you put in your aquarium because these bugs can capture tadpoles, frogs, and even small fish! If you collect adult water bugs, be sure you put a lid on your aquarium so they cannot fly out.

How long can water scorpions and toe biters stay underwater? Some aquatic insects have gills to take in oxygen from the water, and they can remain underwater for their entire lives. Other aquatic insects must return to the surface to breathe.

Bring a timer, a notebook, and pen with you into the field. Watch any aquatic insect that returns to the surface to take a breath. Water scorpions, back-swimmers, water boatmen, and mosquito larvae are good choices. Time how long they can stay underwater.

Can larger animals stay underwater for longer amounts of time? Can fast-swimming toe biters stay under longer than slow-moving water scorpions?

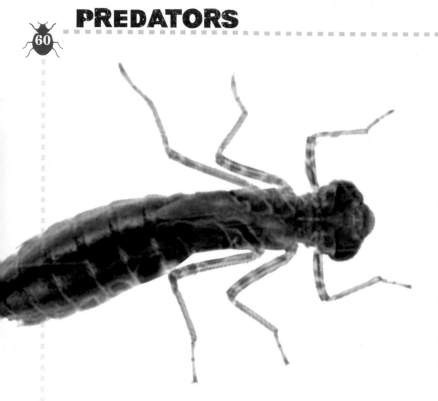

Looking at this damselfly naiad, you can see the labium and mandible. Check out the three leaf-like gills that are not on dragonfly naiads.

UNDERWATER Dragons!

Other voracious predators often collected in ponds and lakes are dragonfly naiads. These predators have specialized mouthparts for grabbing their prey. Remember the chewing mouthparts of insects? (See page 9.) The labia of dragonfly naiads are hinged and are normally tucked under their heads. When a naiad sees prey and is ready to strike, it squeezes its abdomen, which forces "blood" into its lower lip. The higher blood pressure causes the lip to expand and shoot out in front of the naiad, helping it grab prey with its teeth. The naiad holds the prey with its labium and chews it up with its mandibles. Adult dragonflies live on land and fly through the air.

Dragonfly naiad using its labium to catch fish prey

The naiad of a dragonfly is totally aquatic.

When dragonflies become adults, the naiads climb out of the water and molt.

Naiads are totally aquatic. They live and breathe underwater, and their gills are in their butts! Watch them closely and you can see them pump water in and out of their abdomens. They can use this pumping action to move. Just like they squeeze their abdomens to create pressure for moving their mouthparts, they can also use this pressure to force water out of their butts to swim with jet propulsion.

When they are ready to become adults, naiads climb out of

the water and molt. The newly emerged adults have soft exoskeletons and folded wings. After molting, adults must hang from branches while their bodies pump blood into their wings and their new exoskeletons harden.

Dragonfly naiad

Adult dragonfly

POLLINATORS

NO FLOWERS
without Pollinators

Sometimes, wind moves plant pollen, but most flowering plants need helpers. Animal partners such as birds, mammals, and insects that move pollen are called pollinators. It seems very nice of animals, including insects, to pollinate flowers. Why do you think they do this?

Insects visit flowers to eat nectar and pollen. Plants make their showy petals, fragrance, andsugary nectar to attract pollinators. Some social insects bring this food back to their nests, so that others can eat it. Pollen is like powdery dust — it sticks to everything it touches.

This honeybee is covered in pollen.

While an insect is eating or collecting nectar and pollen, it is being coated in more pollen. Insects and other pollinators carry pollen from flower to flower because they can't help it!

Fruits & Nuts

What's your favorite fruit? Do you like blueberries, apples, or melons? How about nuts, like hazelnuts, pecans, or almonds? Hazelnuts are fruits, and pecans and almonds are the seeds of fruits. What about chocolate? Chocolate is made from cocoa beans, which are the seeds of fruits!

Where does fruit come from? Plants make flowers and fruits to reproduce — to make more plants.

Try reading the next paragraph while looking at the flower drawing. Look for each flower part.

First, a flower is pollinated — that is, pollen is moved from a flower's anther to a flower's stigma. Can you find an anther and stigma on the illustration? Better yet, try and find them on a real flower. When a single grain of pollen reaches the sticky stigma of a flower, it does amazing things. First, it makes a tiny, tiny tube that reaches all the way down to the flower's ovule, inside the ovary.

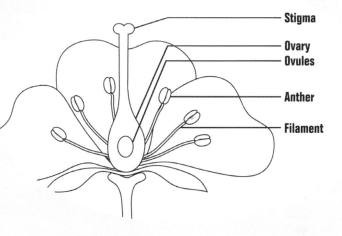

Stigma
Ovary
Ovules
Anther
Filament

The pollen grain also sends two cells down the tube. This step is when fertilization happens: one cell fertilizes an egg in the ovule, and this will become the new plant. The other cell that travels down the tube helps make food for the new plant, inside the seed.

Now that you understand pollination, we can think about chocolate again. Did you know that tiny flies called midges are the pollinators for cocoa?

Pollinators & PLANTS

What insect pollinators can you name? Think for a minute.

Maybe you said the honeybee. Farmers use honeybees to pollinate crops. However, honeybees are not the only kind of bees that pollinate plants. For example, in North America, there are more than 4,000 other kinds of bees, and many of them pollinate plants!

Most bees are hairy. These hairs trap pollen and may be on the thorax, abdomen, or legs. On some bees, the hairs form baskets on their legs or abdomens. Bees come in many sizes and colors!

Some scientists study which insects pollinate which plants. Other scientists study how things humans do, such as farming and gardening, affect insect pollinators. For example, a butterfly garden attracts different pollinators than a vegetable garden. Why do you think this is true?

Honeybee

Bees have pollen baskets.

Bumble bee

This tiny bee pollinates squash blossoms.

Different Colors and Odors Attract Different Pollinators

What are your favorite flowers? Do you like violets? Magnolias? Sunflowers? How do these flowers differ? Can you name a flower that is usually red or orange? Can you name one that has a strong smell? You can use flower color, shape, and smell to predict the kind of insect that pollinates a plant.

• Bees often pollinate yellow, blue, or purple flowers with strong, sweet smells. These flowers sometimes have ultraviolet patterns, in addition to the colors you can see! Bees can see colors in the range between ultraviolet and orange, but cannot see red.

• Butterflies often pollinate bright red or orange flowers with sweet smells. They see bright colors with their compound eyes, but they taste with receptors on their feet! Butterflies suck nectar from flowers with long tubes.

• Most moths pollinate flowers with pale colors that smell strongest at night, when most moths are active.

• Beetles often pollinate large, pale flowers with strong smells.

• Flies often pollinate flowers with drab colors, like maroon or brown, and smells that we do not find attractive. For example, a flower pollinated by flies might smell like rotting meat!

Bug Camp Experiment

Have Fun Watching Pollinators

An important first step when doing any kind of science is to observe. Make a datasheet or label a page in your notebook with the information to the right.

Date/ Time	Flower Color	Pollinator	What I Saw
3 May 11 am	Yellow	Honeybee	Pollen on its legs
4 May 9 am	Purple	Bumble Bee Small Red Beetle	Bee was buzzing loudly

Find a flowering plant or a garden patch. Observe and write down which insects visit which flowers. Remember that common insect pollinators are bees, beetles, flies, butterflies, and moths. Depending on your location and the season, you might also see hummingbirds!

If you need help identifying your insects, look through pages 12–21 to review important traits. An insect identification book and a hand lens or a microscope may also be helpful.

Do Pollinators Have Favorite Colors?

What did you observe? Which kinds of insects did you see most often at yellow flowers? How about red flowers? If you only saw bees at yellow flowers, it would be tempting to say the color yellow attracts bees. However, there might be something else about those flowers that the bees really like, such as the smell! Let's do an experiment to figure out whether colors, and only colors, can attract insect pollinators.

What you need

12 plastic bowls of the same size and shape in four different colors (3 in each color)
Liquid dish soap

What to do

1 Place the bowls in a group that has one bowl of each color.

2 Set up two more groups of bowls in different places. Why do you think this is important?

3 Fill each bowl about halfway with water and add a few drops of dish detergent.

4 Check your bowls in a few hours or the next day. Make sure all the bowls are left out for the same amount of time.

5 Now you can identify the insects in each bowl! Make a datasheet like the one you made for your observations, but this time, try a format like the one here.

6 Look over your data. What do you think? Are insects attracted to only color? What happens if you repeat the experiment with a spoon of sugar mixed in the water instead of dish soap?

Do honeybees only like yellow flowers? Do this experiment to find out.

Date	Bowl Location	Bowl Color	Insects Collected
3 May	Grass next to house	White	Beetle Beetle Bee
3 May	Back porch	White	Small moth Beetle

SYMBIOSIS

Some of the insects you've read about live together with other species. For example, ants protect aphids, treehoppers, and some caterpillars from predators. Some ants even keep aphid eggs in their ant nests during the winter, to shelter them. When spring comes, the ants carry the young aphids back to their host plants. Why do you think ants do all of these things? The type of relationship that ants have with these other insects is called a symbiosis. A symbiosis is when two or more species live closely together. Read about different kinds of symbioses below.

MUTUALISM

Have you ever seen ants attracted to sweet foods or liquids such as spilled soda? Insects such as aphids and treehoppers have mouths like tiny straws, and puncture plants with their mouth-parts to feed on sugary sap. Just like other animals, insects excrete waste: they pee. Because aphids and treehoppers feed on sugary sap, their waste is also very sugary, and entomologists call it honeydew. Ants farm aphids to collect honeydew — just like people farm cows to collect milk. When an ant is ready to collect honeydew, it strokes the aphid or the treehopper with its antennae. This relationship between ants and aphids is good for both species, so it's called a mutualism. The ants get honeydew, and the aphids are protected from predators. Mutualisms occur between all kinds of living organisms.

Have you ever eaten figs? Figs look like fruit, but are really inside-out clusters of tiny flowers. How do flowers hidden inside the plant get pollinated? Fig flowers have a smell that attracts female wasps. The wasps crawl through small holes in the figs to the flowers inside. It is a tight fit! As they squeeze through, their wings are pulled off. Once inside, females pollinate the flowers with pollen from the fig where they grew up. Females lay eggs in some of the flowers. The eggs hatch, the larvae eat the plant's tissues, and they grow to become adults. After mating, females leave to find other figs. In this mutualism, the figs get pollinated and the wasps get shelter and food for their young.

PARASITISM

Not all symbioses are good for both partners. Parasitism is good for one partner but bad for the other partner. Female mosquitoes, lice, and fleas are insects that feed on host animals, and this is not good for the hosts. What other parasites can you think of?

Flea

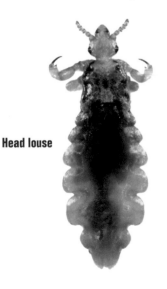

Head louse

Tick

Wow, a Three-Partner Mutualism!

Termites feed on wood. Wood is some of the toughest material on earth! Termites cannot digest wood without help. Inside a termite's gut live single-celled organisms called protists. The protists break down the wood, but the protists need help, too. Inside the protists are bacteria. The bacteria make an enzyme that breaks down lignin and cellulose, the stuff that makes wood tough. This mutualism has three partners: bacteria inside a protist that's inside a termite!

Another parasitoid is the larva of a wasp called the cicada killer. This very large wasp may look scary, but female cicada killers are not interested in you. They feed on nectar and they hunt cicadas for their young. A female cicada killer digs a burrow with several cells in the soil. She finds and paralyzes a cicada that may be three times her body weight. She picks it up, carries it back to the burrow, and places it in a cell, where she lays an egg on it. When the egg hatches, her larva will eat the paralyzed cicada.

Cicada killer

PARASITOIDS

Some parasites kill their hosts. These parasites are called parasitoids. Many parasitoids are wasps that lay their eggs on or inside other insects while the other insects are still alive. When the eggs hatch, the wasp larvae feed on the host insect and kill it.

One kind of parasitoid wasp lays its eggs inside of hornworm caterpillars that you can find on tomato plants. You can tell if a hornworm has been parasitized if it is covered in white wasp pupae.

Flies can also be parasitoids. In fact, there is a whole family of flies that are parasitoids of crickets, katydids, leaf-footed bugs, and many other kinds of insects. Flies in this group have evolved cool adaptations for finding their hosts. They eavesdrop on the sounds or smells their hosts use to talk to each other. The fly shown below uses smells to find hemipteran hosts.

Hornworm caterpillar with wasp pupae

Parasitoid fly

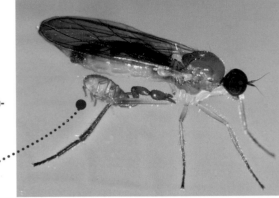

This pseudo-scorpion is hitchhiking on this fly.

COMMENSALISM

Some symbioses are called commensalisms. They are good for one partner, but not good or bad for the other partner. One common example of an insect commensalism is hitchhiking. Some tiny invertebrates can't fly, but they need to get to food. Flower mites and pseudo-scorpions are tiny, flightless invertebrates that hitch rides on flying insects. This hitchhiking doesn't appear to harm the insect, and can help the hitchhiker.

Science on the Move

In tropical forests, army ants search for other insects to eat in great, long swarms made from thousands of ants. Army ants always move in big groups, and they move often. They even bring their queen and brood with them. As they move, many insects, spiders, and other invertebrates fly up or scatter to escape. It's just like when insects scatter as you walk through a field, but imagine many, many more insects.

Some birds in Central and South America follow army ant raids through the forests. These birds eat insects that are trying to get away from the army ants. In fact, some bird species get most of their food by following army ants.

For a long time, many scientists thought this symbiosis was a commensalism — good for the birds, and not bad for the ants. However, some scientists recently found that when army ants are followed by birds, the ants collect less food. Based on this study, this symbiosis seems like parasitism. This is another example of cool science changing what we know . . . or what we think we know!

INSECTS in HIDING

Insects are pretty small and are prey for many animals. It is no wonder that insects have evolved so many cool adaptations to help protect themselves from predators.

CAMOUFLAGE

One of the best ways to avoid being eaten is to hide. Some insects hide under rocks or logs. Some insects burrow into the ground. Other insects hide in plain view by using camouflage. They blend into the area around them or look like part of their environment.

The walking sticks are great examples of insect camouflage. Watch a walking stick move. They don't just look like sticks. They act like them, too. Their behavior is unique and deliberate. They walk slowly, swaying their body and legs, and look just like a stick blowing in the wind. Some walking sticks and other insects look like leaves to hide from their predators.

Katydids and grasshoppers are some of the best leaf look-alikes. The wings may even have shapes that look like they have been eaten by caterpillars!

Many katydids and grasshoppers camouflage with leaves. How long do you think it would take you to spot one of these insects if you were out collecting?

These are not sticks!

Bug Camper Tips

Many camouflaged insects are active and easily spotted at night. Search the tops of plants with a headlight.

This is not bird poop!

Some insects look like sticks (top left and top right), bark (bottom left), and even bird poop (bottom right).

Monarch adults and larvae use bright colors to tell predators they are poisonous.

WARNING COLORS

Some insects do not hide at all. In fact, they sport bright, showy colors and they are easily seen. Think about the road signs you see every day. Yellow, red, orange, and black are often used with traffic warnings. It is the same for insects and other animals. Their colors say, "STOP, DON'T EAT ME!"

Have you ever wondered why monarch butterflies or bees are so bright? Their colors tell other animals that they taste bad or can cause harm. When birds bite into monarchs, many of them get sick from poisons in the monarch's blood. Where does the poison come from? Remember that monarch caterpillars eat milkweed, which has a poisonous sap. The caterpillars add some of this poison to their blood. Their bright colors warn predators of the poison and protect caterpillars from being eaten.

MIMICS

Some insects use bright colors to hide among the poisonous and harmful insects! These copycats are called mimics. Many beetles, flies, and moths look just like wasps or bees so that birds will not eat them. How can you tell them apart? Don't be fooled. Just look at their mouthparts, antennae, and wings and you should not have any problems knowing which insects are bees and wasps and which insects are copycats.

Bumble bee or copycat moth? Look at the antennae to find out!

Look at these two hover flies. One looks like a yellow jacket (top) and the other, a bee (below). If you look closely, you can see that they are true flies with only two wings and short antennae. Wasps and bees have four wings and elbowed antennae.

EYESPOTS

Have you ever wondered why some insects have shapes that look like eyes on their wings? These are not really eyes and the insects do not use them to see. If you happen to find an insect with eyespots, such as the Io moth above, it will probably have its eyes hidden behind its front wings.

If you pretend you're a predator and use your finger to peck at the Io moth like a bird, the moth will open up its wings to reveal the eye-

Eyespots may confuse or startle predators.

spots underneath. The eyespots might startle you. They might startle a bird, too, and help save the moth's life.

Also, when birds and other predators attack insects, they often aim for their heads. Eyespots might protect some moths because birds grab them on the wings instead of their heads. The wings can tear and the moths can escape.

INSECTS in the DARK

Many insects are nocturnal and are only active after the sun goes down. The idea of collecting insects at night can be a little scary, but once you get outside you will be amazed at the different kinds and numbers of insects you see. And, you will notice how different they are from the ones you find in the daytime. They are easy to find: just search on and around plants with a flashlight or a headlight.

BEETLES

Nighttime is also when you can experience those insects that create their own light. Some of the more spectacular light displays are produced by fireflies. Usually the males fly and flash their lights as they search for mates. Each species has its own flash pattern code. Females perched on the ground or on vegetation will answer the males of their own species with a flash. Pairs flash back and forth as the males fly to the females. Then they mate.

It is not always a bed of roses in the world of firefly mating. Females of some species are copycats. They answer the males of other species to lure them to their sides. Then, they EAT THEM!

How can you tell that fireflies are beetles? Look closely at their front wings for a clue. How do they hold their wings when they fly?

A third kind of beetle, the railroad worm, also glows. Females never get wings, and they still look like the larvae after they pupate. Adult males have wings and very large antennae. In this group, the flying males find females using smell. When disturbed, females curl up into a ball and glow, which may warn predators that they taste bad.

Some click beetles also use light when searching for mates. Look for paired light organs on the segment just behind their head.

A railroad worm female in defense mode

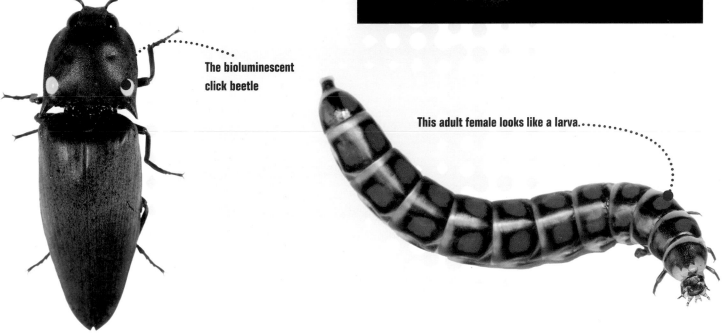

The bioluminescent click beetle

This adult female looks like a larva.

Have Fun with Fireflies

There are lots of ways to observe and experiment with fireflies. Here are a few ideas.

• Study the flash codes of some nearby fireflies. If you can figure out their pattern, you can copy their flash patterns with an LED and attract the males right to you. It may take a little practice because you have to get the timing just right. Since each species has its own flash code, the pattern you find in one place might be very different than the pattern in another place.

• Capture some fireflies. Find their light organs on the undersides of their abdomens, near the tip.

• At some times of the year, you may see many glowing lights on the ground. Track them down and you may find firefly larvae. The larvae look and act very different from the adults. They live in soil and eat other insects, snails, and earthworms.

Male fireflies attracted to a glowing LED

Firefly larva

FLIES

Some insects use their lights to attract prey. The larvae of some fungus gnats glow, and their light attracts small flies and other nocturnal flying insects. The larvae live in silk webs covered with sticky droplets. When flying insects get stuck in the droplets, the glowworms eat them!

Another type of glowworm lives in the Waitomo caves in New Zealand. The larvae of these flies catch prey in glowing, sticky mucus that hangs down from the cave ceilings.

SOCIAL INSECTS

Many kinds of insects live in groups. Have you ever seen a line of ants moving on the ground? What other insects have you seen in groups? Some insects live in groups all the time, and some insects live in groups for just a little while. Some insects never live in groups at all.

SOME DO, Some don't

Dragonflies and damselflies never live in groups.

Some insects, such as these stink bugs, live in groups while they are young, but live alone as adults.

Some insects form groups during the day, but search for food alone at night.

Some insects, such as these bees, live in groups all the time.

Families Come in Many Forms!

When you think of insect groups, you might think of the truly social insects first. All ants and termites, many bees, some wasps, and some beetles and aphids are social insects. In these species, groups share a nest and only one or a few adults (queens) reproduce. Nests also house many other females (workers and sometimes soldiers), and sometimes one or more males. The workers do not reproduce, but they take care of the brood. (The brood includes eggs, larvae, and pupae.) Often, there will be insects from several generations in one nest.

Earwig mother with eggs and nymphs

Adult ants caring for brood

Many other kinds of insects live in family groups, but they differ in one or more ways from social insects. Earwig mothers clean their eggs, feed their nymphs, and protect eggs and nymphs from predators, but they nest by themselves, not with many other earwig females.

What Do Insects Do in Groups?

STAY ALIVE!

A group of insects has many eyes with which to see predators. Many insects that live in groups also defend themselves with chemicals. A group can pack a bigger punch!

There is power in numbers! Sawfly larvae cluster together and defend each other.

Oleander aphids (below) and giant honeybees (below right) live in large groups. When predators attack from the air, the insects closest to the predator lift up and then drop back down as a group over and over again. Nearby aphids or bees feel the up-down motion happening, so they do it too, but just a tiny bit later. The whole group looks as though it is rippling, very much like people who are "doing the wave" at a sports stadium!

Above: Treehopper nymphs "do the wave" to tell their mother where a sneaky predator is attacking. She defends her young and then signals them to be quiet.

Above: Japanese honeybees and giant honeybees form clusters or balls around predators such as hornets that land on the nest. Each bee uses the flight muscles in its thorax to produce heat. Together, all the bees raise the temperature inside the "beeball" to 45 °C (113 °F) or more, and they cook the hornet!

FIND AND EAT FOOD!

Parents feed their young. Earwig mothers vomit food for their nymphs, and burying beetle parents bury a dead animal with their eggs, so their young will have plenty to eat.

Some treehopper nymphs feed in groups on tender new plant leaves. When a leaf grows old, the treehoppers start stamping and marching in place. A few nymphs leave the group to wander. When one of them finds a new, tender leaf, it sends vibrations through the stem to tell the other treehoppers where to go.

Treehopper nymphs

Below: Ants capture and carry large prey by working together in a group. Have you ever seen ants working together to carry something?

FIND NEW HOMES!

Social insects start new nests and colonies. Sometimes a queen starts a new nest by herself, but sometimes many workers come along with her, as in the honeybee swarm shown above. Have you ever seen a bee swarm?

STAY WARM AND KEEP COOL!

Social insects cannot let their brood get too cold or too hot. Bees, wasps, ants, and termites can increase their nest's temperature just by bunching together! To warm their brood, bees also shiver their flight muscles, and some wasps blow warm air from their tracheae. To cool their nests down, bees and wasps fan their wings.

Tent caterpillars tell group-mates where to find food by laying down chemical trails.

In Australia, spitfire sawfly larvae feed on trees in small groups at night. They merge into large groups to move from one tree to another, forming long chains. Biologist Lynn Fletcher found that when a spitfire larva is separated from the group, it taps its "butt" on the tree or ground. The other spitfires tap back, and the lost spitfire searches for and finds them!

Below left: A large group of spitfire sawfly larvae on a tree trunk in Australia

Right and below right: Spitfire sawfly larvae feeding on a plant

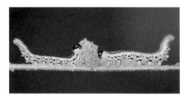

Bug Camp Experiment

Have Fun Experimenting with Ant Baiting

Ant colonies can be very large. Workers have to bring home enough food for everyone in the colony. How long does it take for an ant colony to find food? How do scouts show their nest mates where to find food? You can answer these questions by baiting ants with food! Ant baiting works best on sunny, warm days.

What you need

Index cards or pieces of paper
Bait such as honey or maple syrup, peanut butter, a cookie, or canned meat
    (tuna fish and SPAM® work well)
Notebook or data sheet
Pencil

What to do

1 Read through the steps below. Predict how long it will take before ants find your bait. Predict how many ants you will see when you check the bait after 15 minutes, 30 minutes, and 45 minutes.

2 Set up your notebook or data sheet to look like the chart at the upper right.

Date	Bait	Time	Where	Ant Types	How Many
7 June	Peanut Butter	1 pm	Soil Near House	Small, Black	1
		1:15 pm		Small, Black	3
		1 pm	Soil Near Sidewalk	Large, Red	1
		1:15 pm		Large, Red	1

3 To set up your baits, put the same amount of food in the middle of at least two index cards. Choose a baiting place such as a building, a yard, or a garden. Place the cards on the ground at least a few steps away from each other. Note the time and then walk away.

4 Check your baits every 15 minutes for one hour. Count the ants when you check the baits and write down the total number of ants you find. Don't collect the ants when you check the baits!

5 Look at the data in your notebook. Think about the predictions you made in Step 1. Did your predictions match your results? You might want to show your results in a graph with minutes on the x-axis and the number of ants on the y-axis. If you do this experiment again, how will you change it?

Bug Camper Tip

Ants often stay close to other insects that live in groups, such as aphids and treehoppers. By keeping an eye out for ants and following them, you might find other insect groups!

How Do Ants Find Food?

Some ants tell their nest mates where food is by putting a chemical trail on the ground. Other ants bring their nest mates to the food, one at a time. (If you see pairs of ants running together, this might be what's going on.) Some ants do both of these things. Observe the ants closely. What do you see?

If you see a line of ants or ants that look like they are following a trail, try putting a piece of paper over part of the trail. What do you predict will happen? What do you predict will happen if you wait 15 minutes and then turn the paper sideways? Try it and see!

Male house cricket using his wings to make sound

Many insects make sounds by rubbing body parts together. When insects make sounds this way, it is called stridulation. Crickets and katydids stridulate with their front wings, while grasshoppers stridulate with their hindlegs.

Watch a male cricket while it chirps. Notice that it holds two wings over its abdomen and scissors them back and forth. Each wing has a file with many teeth and a scraper. When the wings move back and forth, the scraper of one wing pushes across the teeth of the other wing's file. These movements cause the wing membranes to vibrate, making sound. The file and scraper only touch when the wings close, so each wing movement cycle makes a single sound pulse.

Crickets can move their wings back and forth very fast — more than one hundred times per second in some species! (How many times can you clap your hands or snap your fingers in one second?) It may be hard to see single wing movements. Listen carefully, can you hear more than one pulse of sound in a chirp or trill?

GAME Time!

You can learn a lot about the signals of crickets and other nocturnal insects by playing sound games with your friends. Ask an adult or someone who does not want to play to be the referee.

1 Find a partner! Everyone should form pairs in a large field or gym. Give each pair a hair comb, a pencil, and two blindfolds.

2 Each pair will pretend to be a type of cricket. Because different cricket species make different signals, each pair must come up with a unique sound. To make a sound, pull the pencil across the comb. (If you're thinking like a cricket, imagine the pencil is a scraper and the comb is a file.) While you're making practice sounds, think about what makes a good signal. Is it loud to reach long distances? Or always the same? Or very different from other sounds? All three? You have five minutes to come up with your signal.

3 Ask each pair to decide who will be the signaler and who will be the receiver. When the game starts, the signaler will stand still and make the pair's sound, while the receiver will move around. Sound easy? Remember that crickets are nocturnal.

4 To make it seem like nighttime, tie your blindfolds in place. No peeking and no talking until the game is over! **Safety Note:** Move slowly and carefully when blindfolded. Referees need to look

out for potential collisions and trip hazards.

5 Start moving around until everyone is separated and the referee yells, "Let the signaling begin!" The game ends when a receiver finds his or her signaler.

6 After you've played the game a few times, talk with your friends about your signals. How easy was it to find your partners? Would you choose a different signal next time?

7 Sometimes predators or parasites use signals to find their prey or host. Add a blindfolded predator or parasite to your game. The pair loses if the signaler attracts a parasite or predator before it attracts a mate. How does this change whether a signal works well?

The snowy tree cricket is known as the thermometer cricket because you can figure out the temperature by counting its chirps.

Have Fun Recording Insect Sounds

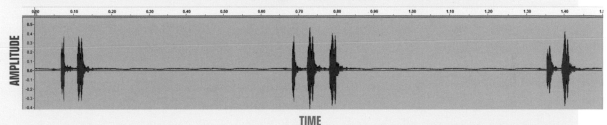

You can use any kind of recording device to record the sound of a singing insect. While a cricket is making sound, use a voice recorder app on a cell phone or computer to record it. These apps make pictures of the sound that show the timing and loudness of an insect's song. Each pulse of sound is a single wing cycle. The male house cricket in the picture above left of page 88 moved its wings twice during the first and third chirp and three times during the second chirp.

It is important to record the temperature whenever you record insect sounds because they move much slower when it's cold, which changes their sound. A hot cricket, for example, moves its wings much faster than a cold cricket.

MOVING INSECTS

Have you ever noticed that if you leave your porch light on, insects will fly to it? Porch lights are a great way to catch some nighttime insects. It is also an example of what biologists call taxis. A taxis is a behavior where an animal moves toward or away from something.

In the porch light example above, light is the stimulus and insects fly toward it. When an animal moves toward a stimulus, the response is positive. Some insects, such as roaches, move away from light, which is a negative response. The word phototaxis describes responses to light. Moths show positive phototaxis, and roaches show negative phototaxis.

Think about taxis for a minute. Would you show positive or negative taxis to a huge slice of chocolate cake? Ten hours of homework? A cute puppy? Animals move toward and away from many kinds of things.

Type of Stimulus	Prefix	Word Used to Describe It
Light	Photo	Phototaxis
Sound	Phono	Phonotaxis
Chemical	Chemo	Chemotaxis
Magnetism (from earth's magnetic fields)	Magneto	Magnetotaxis
Gravity	Geo	Geotaxis
Touch	Thigmo	Thigmotaxis
Current (wind or water)	Rheo	Rheotaxis

Experiment with PHOTOTAXIS

Fireflies make and respond to light signals. In the field, females stay in one place and answer the flash signals of flying males. When male fireflies respond and move toward flashing females, that is positive phototaxis. Males and females take turns flashing, and the amount of time between a male's signal and a female's answer is different for each species.

You can study phototaxis by looking for females in the field. Watch as they respond to the signals of nearby males. Use a stopwatch to measure the time between the beginning of the male's signal and the female's answer. Is the time always the same? If so, you can use a small penlight to answer males with the timing you observed. Can you attract males to your hand?

Cockroach Mazes

You can measure phototaxis in a cockroach with a T or Y maze. A cockroach will walk down the runway and choose between a lighted tunnel in one direction and a darkened tunnel in the other direction. Which direction do you think it will choose?

To make your own maze, build runways with cardboard and tape or with building blocks such as Legos. You can make the walls as high as you like, and you can cover it with a thin piece of clear plastic or plastic wrap. Use a red light when you run your experiment, and use a small flashlight on one end of your maze.

T-Maze

Dark ← · · · · · · · · → Light

Start

This T-maze is made with black cardboard.

THINK LIKE A SCIENTIST

Biologists use mazes to test what kinds of decisions are made by many kinds of animals. When doing experiments, scientists like to repeat the same experiment many times because sometimes things happen just by chance. If your roach chose the light side of the maze, how do you know it chose that side because of the light and not because of chance? Since you gave your roach two choices — lightness and darkness — there was a 50 percent chance it would have turned to the light even if you had blindfolded it. The solution to this problem is to repeat many trials of the same experiment.

Maybe your cockroach turned toward the light because it liked that direction, and not because it wanted to be closer to the light. The solution to this problem is to randomize the light and dark sides. One way to randomize would be to flip a coin for each run of the maze. If the coin lands heads side up, place the dark option on the right side. If the coin lands tails side up, place the dark option on the left side.

Check Your Messages: Phonotaxis

Some animals use signals to find members of their own species for mating. When males (or females) make a signal, the other sex moves toward them. For instance, the chirp of a male cricket attracts females that either walk or fly toward the singing male. Their movement is an example of positive phonotaxis.

You can explore phonotaxis in crickets by recording the song of a male and playing it back to a female. Capture some field crickets either by homing in on their calling song or by looking under logs and rocks. Female crickets use a long, spear-like organ that sticks out of their abdomen to move eggs out of their bodies. Put the males in a small wire cage and record them when they rub their wings together to make sounds. Remember that each species has its own song. Will females respond to the songs of males from a different species? To find out, record the songs of two different cricket species and play them for females.

Keep Current: Rheotaxis

You can see rheotaxis in stream insects such as mayflies. Go to a stream and lift up flat rocks to find some large mayflies. Place the rock in the current so you can watch the mayflies. Do they face upstream or downstream? Now, slowly spin the rock so they face a different direction. Does the mayfly change its direction relative to the stream's current? Why do you think they face the direction they do?

Investigating mayflies in a stream can help you to understand rheotaxis.

Have Fun Experimenting with Thigmotaxis

Place an insect in a square container and watch it. Measure how much time it spends next to the wall and how much time it spends away from the wall. Even though there is more space in the center of the container, most insects will spend the majority of time along the walls. This is positive thigmotaxis. Why might it be important for insects to respond to touch in this way? Is there an advantage to being next to something sturdy in the wild?

ACKNOWLEDGMENTS

I want to thank Herb Pomfrey, who collaborated with me on bug camps during so many summers; the Burroughs Wellcome Fund for providing much-appreciated camp funding; and the little "buggers" we taught. I also thank John Tripp, Tom Walker, Jim Lloyd, and Ron Hoy for their excitement and enthusiasm about the science of insects, and Linda Block for helpful manuscript suggestions. I appreciate the hard work of Dawn Cusick and Susan McBride who made this book fun. Finally, thanks mom, for always letting me explore — little did you know that was the start of my entomological career.

— Tim Forrest

I thank Tim Forrest and Herb Pomfrey for introducing me to bug camp, many years ago! Thanks to the biologists who have shared their love of nature with me and involved me in wonderful field experiences. Tim, Rex Cocroft, and Christine Miller mentored me as a biologist and educator. I thank Susan McBride and Dawn Cusick for their patience and hard work, and for making this project a wonderful experience. Finally, thanks to my parents for encouraging me to play in the woods and streams. Biologists never grow up.

— Jen Hamel

The authors would like to thank the following illustrators and photographers for their creative contributions.
Joseph Berger/Bugwood.org/Creative Commons (page 88-top left); Ronald F. Billings/Texas A&M/Forest Service/Bugwood.org (page 70-upper right); BlueDawe/Wickimedia Commons (page 86-bottom right); Andrew C./Wickimedia (page 70-bottom right), Clemson University/USDA Cooperative Extension Slide Series/Bugwood.org (page 55-bottom); Rex Cocroft (page 85-bottom); Stephen Dalton/Getty Images (page 28-top); Jeff Delonge/Creative Commons (page 32-middle left); S. Dennis (page 84-top); T.G. Forrest (pages 27-bottom left, 28-top and bottom left, 29-left, 35-bottom, 36-top right, 38-bottom and top, 39-bottom left, 42-top right, 43-top left, top right, and bottom, 44-above top left, top right, and below, 45-above and below, 46-top left and bottom right, 47, 48-left, 50-top right, 51-top, 66-bottom, 67-top right, 75-bottom left, 78-bottom, 80-top right, 81-top, 89-top right and bottom, 92-top left, back cover-center left, middle, and right, and back jacket flap-top); Alex Gorringe/Wickimedia Commons (page 86-bottom left); Jen Hamel (pages 17-top center and top left, 19-middle left and right, 64-middle right, 82-middle left, 84-top, and back jacket flap-bottom); London Scientific Films/Getty (page 60-bottom right); Dan Mele (pages 25-bottom right, 34-top right, and 79-top right); Tom Oates (page 83-top); Sarefo/Creative Commons (page 71-top); Adam Sisson/Iowa State University/Bugwood.org (page 82-middle right); Takahashi/Wickimedia Commons (page 84-bottom right); S. E. Thorpe/Wickimedia Commons (page 23-top right); Waitomo Glowworm Caves/New Zealand (page 81-bottom); and Christian Ziegler/Getty Images (page 71-bottom left)

From Shutterstock: 5 Second Studio, Accurate Shot, Zuhairi Ahmad, Alexsvirid, Alle, Brandon Alms, Alslutsky, Protasov An, Anatolich, Calvin Ang, Antonsov85, Aodaodaodaod, Arsgera, Asharkyu, Juan Aunion, Evgeniy Ayupov, Nancy Bauer, Radu Bercan, Hagit Berkovich, Blue Ring Media, Blur Life 1975, BMCL, Aleksander Bolbot, Ryan M. Bolton, Stephen Bonk, Steve Bower, Boyphare, Alena Brozova, Edwin Butter, Caimacanul, Joseph Calev, Captiva55, Chanachola, Suede Chen, Katarina Christenson, Cindy Creighton, Corlaffra, Cynoclub, Nicola Dal Zotto, Nathan B. Dappen, Gerald A. DeBoer, Angel DiBilio, Dog Box Studio, Dynamicfoto, EEO, Ehtesham, Dirk Ercken, Agustin Esmoris, Exopixel, Fablok, Geza Farkas, Melinda Fawver, Fivespots, A.S. Floro, Forest71, Tyler Fox, Watcher Fox, Glenda, Iliuta Goean, Bildagentur Zoonar GmbH, Guy42, Happykamill, Elliotte Rusty Harold, HHelene, Jiang Hongyan, Hopko, Carlos Horta, HTU, Vitalii Hulai, IamTK, Iceink, Infocus, Bogdan Ionescu, Iordanis, Irin-k, IrinaK, Eric Isselee, Sebastian Janicki, Likhit Jansawang, Matt Jeppson, Vaughan Jessnitz, Gregory Johnston, Jps, Sakdinon Kadchiangsaen, Cathy Keifer, Keneva Photography, Anton Kozyrev, Dmitriy Krasko, Kritskaya, Maya Kruchankova, K. Kucharska, D. Kucharski, Kurt_G, Ladyphoto, Hugh Lansdown, Chayatorn Laorattanavech, Henrik Larsson, Doug Lemke, Littlekop, Soloviova Liudmyla, Louella938, Bruce MacQueen, Fabio Maffei, Cosmin Manci, Markh, Mastering Microstock, Mathisa, Cosmin Manci, Medicus, MJTH, Thalerngsak Mongkolsin, MP cz, Narintorn_m2, Maks Narodenko, Aksenova Natalya, Pedro Turrini Neto, Chakkrachai Nicharat, NinaM, NumPhoto, Oksana2010, Fedorov Oleksiy, Nikitina Olga, Bernatskaya Oxana, Padung, Pandapaw, Fabrice Parais, Evgeny Parushin, Somyot Pattana, Paul Reeves Photography, Heiti Paves, Andrey Pavlov, Michael Pettigrew, Photomaster, Photosync, Photowind, Daniel Prudek, Nikola Rahme, Randimal, Morley Read, Rebell, Ian Redding, Aigars Reinholds, Buntoon Rodseng, Paul Rommer, Armin Rose, Jason Patrick Ross, Manfred Ruckszio, R. Runtsch, David Peter Ryan, Peter Schwarz, Schankz, Seeyou, Seregraff, Sergyiway, Guillermo Guerao Serra, Shaftinaction, Ssguy, Starover Sibiriak, Andrew Skolnick, Skoda, Skynetphoto, Angelika Smile, Snapinadil, Somchai Som, QiuJu Song, South 12th Photography, Satit Srihin, Olya Steckel, Steven Russell Smith Photos, Marek R. Swadzba, Johan Swanepoel, Piti Tan, Tetxu, Thatmacroguy, Timquo, Tntphototravis, Tomatito, Marco Uliana, Hector Ruiz Villar, Vchal, Kirsanov Valeriy Vladimirovich, Dennis van de Water, Nick van den Broek, Sphinx Wang, Xfdly, Pan Xunbin, Yaping, Yeko Photo Studio, Feng Yu, and Carlos Yudica

GLOSSARY

Adaptation: A behavior, body part, or ability that helps an organism reproduce more than others of the same species, in the same place

Behavior: The way an organism acts

Camouflage: To blend in with the environment

Community: A biological community includes all the living organisms in one place

DNA: The chemical makeup of an organism's genes

Egg: The first stage of an animal's life cycle that houses the embryo

Exoskeleton: In insects and other arthropods, the strong outer skeleton made from chitin

Habitat: The kind of place that an organism or group of organisms needs for a home

Metamorphosis: The changes in an individual's body form during its life cycle

Molt: In insects and other arthropods, the shedding of an exoskeleton due to growth

Parasite: An organism that feeds on or harms another organism (its host)

Parasitoid: A parasite that kills its host

Phylogeny: A branching tree diagram showing the relationships between taxa. See page 20 for an insect phylogeny.

Predator: An organism that preys on other organisms

Prey: An animal being hunted or eaten by another animal

Species: A group of organisms that can reproduce with each other, but not with other organisms

Symbiosis: Two or more organisms living closely together and interacting

Taxon: A group of organisms that share certain traits. Taxa is the plural form

Toxin: A substance that harms a living organism

ORGANISM INDEX

GENERAL INDEX